FWD: MUSEUMS

IN TRANSIT

Edited by

THERESE QUINN

and

XIMENA MORA Y OLIVÁN

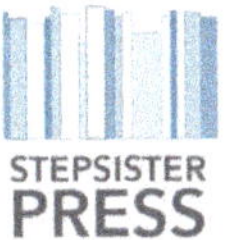

Published by StepSister Press, 600 S. Crescent Avenue, Park Ridge, IL, U.S.A., stepsisterpress.org.

Print ISBN: 978-1-7326989-7-0 — Ebook ISBN 978-1-7326989-8-7

Thank you to our Patreon sponsors for making this publication possible.

Cover art by Larsen Husby.

Interior layout and initial cover concept by Quinton Sledge. Final cover design by Larissa Fardelos.

The interior was formatted in Vellum for print and eBook versions.

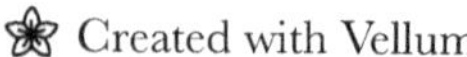 Created with Vellum

ACKNOWLEDGMENTS

With our mission to actively challenge, critique, and reimagine the status quo in the museum world, it is crucial that we acknowledge the colonial narratives and their impact that continue to thrive in the spaces we visit, study, and work within. We stand in solidarity with the voices who strive to de-platform these colonial structures to uplift the Black community, Indigenous community, and people of color.

We thank those who push the boundaries of museum institutions and their historical canons through art, education, activism, and within alternative sites and access points to cultural enrichment.

We share our gratitude to the Museum and Exhibitions Studies (MUSE) Program at UIC, and all program and affiliated faculty who support students seeking to redefine cultural work in the 21st century. A warm thank you to MUSE Director and Fwd: Museums Advisor, Therese Quinn, for her valuable insight and wisdom. Thank you to Annie Heckman, creator of StepSister Press, for her assistance and creative vision in bringing this publication to the hands and screens of our readers, and Lou Barrett, who copy-edited this issue.

A grand thank you to Ximena Mora y Oliván for their active support and guidance to our team as our Publication Coordinator. Thank you to Laura Sato for advising and leading the team's approach to a more accessible publication. Finally, we thank all of the contributors, who endured an impactful transition and made the time to communicate the content of rich ideas, critiques, art, and dialogue.

Abby Foss

Alex Orfirer Maher

Kacie Martinez-Valle

Laura Sato

Loren Wright

Manon Thompson

Quinton Sledge

Ramsey Hoey

Sidney del Ray Murphy

Therese Quinn

Ximena Mora y Oliván

Get to know this year's publication team on the Fwd: Museums website:

https://fwdmuseumsjournal.weebly.com/in-transit-20211.html

CONTENTS

INTRODUCTION

ALEX ORFIRER MAHER & LAURA SATO

Dear Traveler,

Many of us are spending more time in stasis than we could ever want. Others of us are moving through a dangerous world all too frequently. All of us must rethink what it means to be *in transit*. Unintended, we have created a movement arc in our journal. Last year we had *Home*, exploring ideas of comfort, displacement, and physicality. Little did we know that home itself would change entirely during the year it took to produce the journal. Over the course of this year, home has transformed for all of us, becoming both restricting and freeing, work and play, sanctuary and danger.

This year, we have *In Transit*, exploring ideas of transition, transcendence, and transformation. This theme was picked by the team last year while working on Home, but before they realized quite how profound the transition was about to become. Much like we had to reimagine *Home*, we had to reimagine *In Transit*, expanding the definitions and challenging our assumptions. As a team, we wanted the experience of reading this journal to be a journey in itself. We wanted to take you out of the home and into a space of movement, travel, and exploration.

To aid in your journey, we've structured the journal to model a public transit experience. Each piece in this journal is considered a "station" and is organized along a particular "train line." The four train lines are *transport, transition, transformation,* and *transience.* You can follow each train line from the beginning station through to the final destination and then begin on another, or you can transfer at the designated transfer stations to a different train line. Lines and transfer stations are clearly marked on a transit map following the Table of Contents and at the beginning of the transfer piece. We encourage you to explore this journal like you would a new city: take one line through and gaze out the window at the city passing you by or take every transfer you can and get yourself completely lost in a new place. We all know that every good moment of transit is better enjoyed with music. For your listening pleasure, we have crowd-sourced a playlist to get you in the mood, which can be found at the end of the journal. The journey and the experience are yours to shape. Have fun!

We know that transit and transportation have not always been joyful or accessible experiences. We are thinking of you and striving to create a journey that can be enjoyed by all. As scholar and curator Amanda Cachia emphasizes that from access, creativity can occur.[1] To us, access to the journal means that as many people as possible can consume, interact, and engage with the journal and the journey. To help with this, audio recordings of some of the pieces in the journal are provided, and all images have image descriptions. There is also a PDF version of the journal that is screen-reader friendly. We understand that this may still not be enough and that your travels through our journal might still have barriers. If that is the case, please reach out to us as we are always happy to hear ways that we can transform to better suit all needs.

When you have completed your journey with us, you may look back at your home from which you've been transported and perhaps feel sadness or worry in return. But we are here to tell you that there is no return: no "return to normal" or going "back to the way things were." There is only moving forward toward a forever changed reality. The only question we can ask is what do we want that to be? The next step in our journey is *Manifesto*, where we can declare our new position in the world. What can we dream up?

Safe Travels,

Fwd: Museums

LANGUAGE IN TRANSIT

LOREN WRIGHT

In our second issue, *Small*, we included a statement on language by Javairia Shahid entitled "Language Matters."[1] In this issue, we wanted to return to that statement and reiterate the power of language—of "words as worlds," as Shahid put it. Language is not a neutral method of communication—it is powerful and political. What we name, what we allow to go unnamed, and what we include and exclude defines us. Language can deny someone's identity or affirm it; it can open minds or close them. Every word matters. And yet, as the world changes around us and as we change with it, language is changing too. Words and identities are in transit.

With this in mind, we have done our best to be intentional and inclusive with our language choices throughout this issue. We want to be mindful of diverse identities and backgrounds. We imagine our readers to be diverse: e.g., students, academics, workers, people of color, people of varying abilities, queer, straight, trans, and cis. Language isn't perfect, and this journal is not either, but we wrote and edited it with you in mind.

In a few years or less, or more, the language we have carefully chosen will be out of date. There will be new and better ways to name and describe the concepts and identities discussed in this journal. We welcome this as language should change and grow.

GROOVE WHILE ON THE MOVE

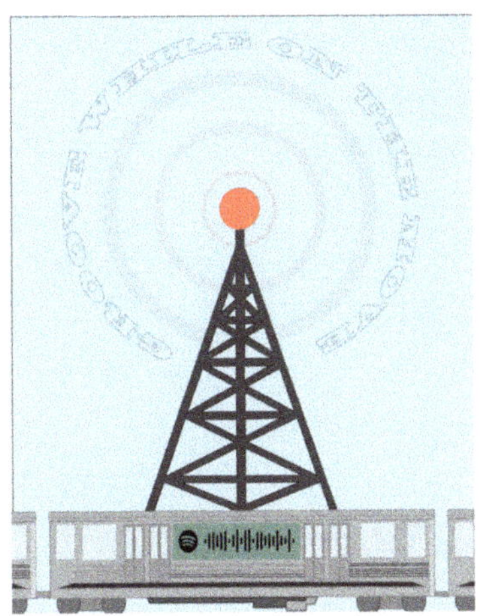

We asked our Instagram followers to share tunes that remind them of what it means to be in a state of transition. Scan the code to access our In Transit Spotify playlist of suggested grooves!

Need help accessing your Spotify code scanner?

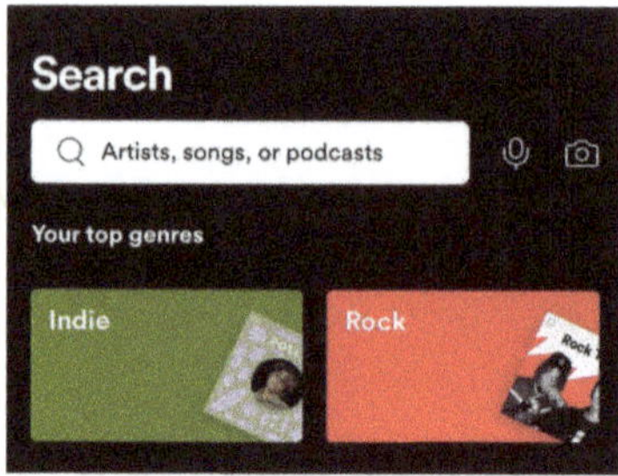

On the right hand corner of the search bar, the CAMERA ICON opens your camera scanner. Scan the green code on the train to enjoy a variety of songs during your transit.

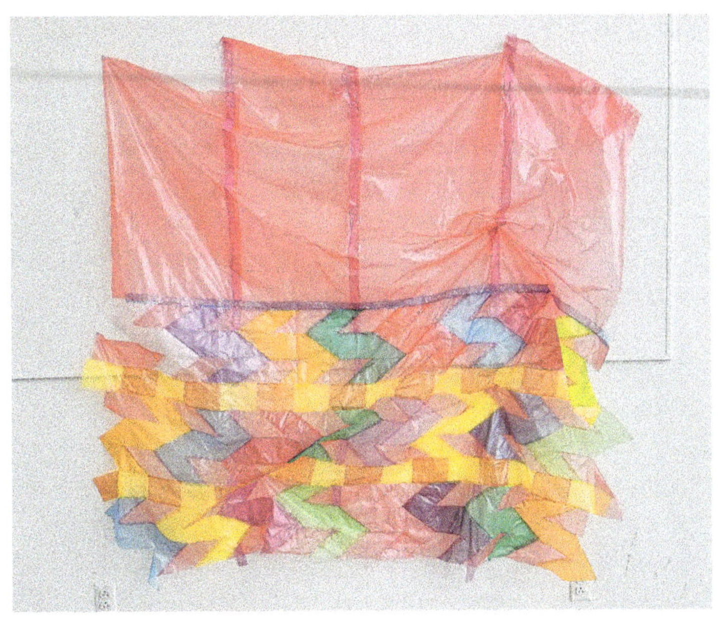

Henry Morales

SEPTA Textile, 2020

Colored Trash Bags 66" X 68"

"MY EXPERIENCE as a first-generation Guatemalan American inspires me to explore themes of labor, immigration, identity, and place through works that mix non-traditional and familiar materials. I am driven to explore what it means to be first-generation, and to investigate the impact of migrating and assimilating to a new place while still holding ties to another land. Another mode in which I explore themes of my identity is through the examination of labor, specifically the labor of my family, and its relation to society's perception of and interactions with them. Through my work, I strive to bring visibility to those who are often ignored by society, and who do not frequently get the opportunity to control their own narrative. My family and our history guide me to share our stories; growing up surrounded by a strong community of hardworking, persistent, and caring people inspires me to celebrate and showcase their experiences. I delve deep into the significance of being a child of immigrants, and through that investigation, aim to honor the lives of my family, culture, heritage, and the impact of these strong people on others. My art incorporates influences from the history of my culture in contrast with modern issues we face; through this, I intend to present the plight of marginalized people while honoring their narrative."

PART 1

TRANSPORT

1

BUY-A-BUS

A PROGRAM FOR THE PUBLIC

SIDNEY DEL RAY MURPHY

I remember being a 5-year-old in the living room, watching *Rick Steve's Europe* on our enormous wooden framed console TV. I dreamed of visiting those places, and of being able to look up at masterpieces. I'd sit with my legs crossed and my nose almost pressed against the glass, wishing for the day I could be in one of those spaces.

My mother and I would wait every month for the free days at the various Seattle-based galleries and museum spaces. We, like many others, couldn't afford the admission fees. Most fees start at $36 a person, not including parking or transportation. These free days were usually the first Thursday of the month, and my mother would get me out of class early so that we didn't hit the rush of other parents and children who had to wait for that one day in the month as well.

I was so young that I couldn't understand all that was being conveyed to me in those pieces, but I knew how they made me feel; the sadness of the faces and the excitement of the colors. I could imagine how the surfaces felt with all the oil paint ridges. I'd follow the paint cracks with my eyes and ask every security guard I could find to tell me about their favorite pieces. I was fully immersed in the artwork, and this one day every month changed my life.

As I began my professional and academic career, the things that I faced as a child came to light. Accessibility and financial ability were now terms that became clear to me, based on the experiences I had going to museums with my mother—not only the admission fees, but having to figure out how to physically get there. We weren't able to afford the high admission prices or the parking, and at times we felt out of place or surveilled in those galleries. My mother knew that these spaces were not designed for us, and that's why we only got that one day. I think a lot about the sacrifices my mother made to allow me to have those experiences and to follow my dreams of working in a museum.

Many children all over the world and in my community were having the same experiences that I had. They could not travel to museums out of state, let alone attend shows in their own cities. The price of admission is too high, parking is expensive, and commuter access is sparse. As a result, many children will never have the chance to see or experience art in a museum space. These spaces can be elitist at times, only promoting themselves to a certain crowd: a crowd that has a car and money to pay for parking, time off to have the luxury of going to a museum, and the ability to pay to get in. The traditional structure of museums was something that bothered me for years, as I worked in many institutions and spaces just like that. It killed me to see young children with their parents turned away, because they didn't have the funds. I had to find a way to participate in a new era and help make changes.

When I began attending Washington State University (WSU) I knew that my goal was to enter the museum field. I began working at the Jordan Schnitzer Museum of Art (JSMOA) on campus, acting as a docent, an intern, and eventually the Special Projects Curator. In this space I was introduced to a program called "Buy A Bus" (BAB)[1]. At that point, BAB[2] had been in practice for about 12 years, serving communities within a 100-mile radius. WSU is in the desert of Eastern Washington, an area made up of many farming communities which were home to low-income and minority families. This area also is and has been home to many First-Nation people including the Nez Perce (Nimi'ipuu) and Palouse (a Sahaptin tribe) whose land was taken to build the University by Land Grant, and surrounding developments. Many students who attend WSU are members of these communities and live within these problematic histories. A program like BAB is aimed to address some of these problems that are present in museum spaces and on university campuses all across the country. The program, which is currently still in operation, will reimburse costs related to schools busing within a 100-mile radius to allow students to attend the museum. Most of these museum trips are by K-12 schools, but they have also reimbursed field trips for seniors, college and university classes, kid's camps, and almost any other request. This program was created in dedication to the museum's ability to evolve offerings to the public, low income areas, and all students while addressing ideas of privilege and elitism in museum spaces.

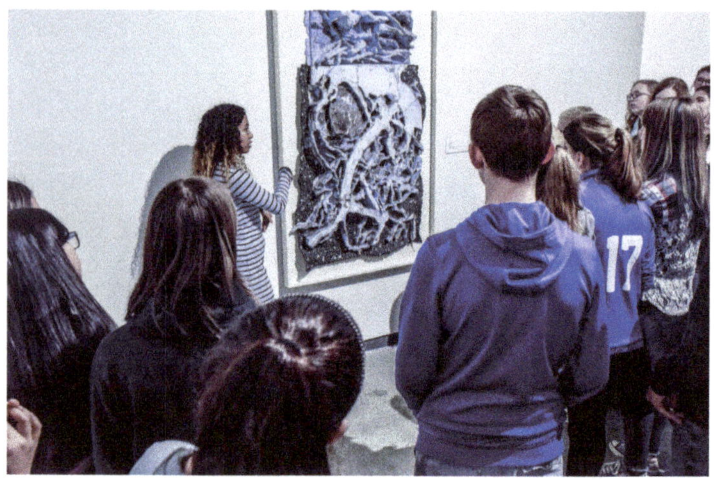

Buy-A-Bus Tour for the 2019 exhibition at the Jordan Schnitzer Museum of Art at WSU, Social Space. This exhibition featured 4 internationally renowned artists; Wangechi Mutu, Leonardo Drew, Julie Mehretu, and Mark Bradford.

When I first became a docent at the museum, I saw first-hand the impact that this program was having on the community. Busloads of students would show up on a weekly basis, and many of the students had not previously seen artwork in person. The younger students were so excited to be in that space that their eyes would dart around trying to take in every inch of the rooms. I would lead these students on critical thinking tours, having them sit in front of pieces to talk about how the colors and shapes made them feel. They were so in tune with the works, and came to conclusions about the art that were so thoughtful. Many students wrote us letters discussing their experience at the museum and how it made them want to work in a space like this one day.

Older students were welcomed into a type of space that many had never visited before, never mind felt comfortable in. Through BAB, they got the opportunity to walk the campus and ask me questions about the college experience. Many ended up reaching out a year or so later to let me know that this experience inspired them to apply for school at WSU, with many receiving funding in art and culture programs.

While one visit and experience in art and cultural space does not fix or begin to tear down the elitist structures of a museum, it does open the door to possibilities of what an accessible space could be like. Students are the future of museums, and the sooner we invite them in and allow them a platform to be creative and think critically about the world around them, the sooner we will see changes in museum structures.

The Buy A Bus program through Washington State University's Jordan Schnitzer Museum of Art is only one example of the amazing progress that cultural workers have been able to make within cultural spaces and the communities those spaces live in. The ability for students to be able to attend museums and cultural spaces should be at the forefront of reimagining institutions and the spaces we live in.

2

HOW WE MOVE

DANIEL TUCKER

When visiting New York City's Central Park you may come across a curious plaque reading:

Here at West 74th Street and Central Park West, Henry H. Bliss dismounted from a streetcar and was struck and knocked unconscious by an automobile on the evening of September 13, 1899. When Mr. Bliss, a New York real estate man, died the next morning from his injuries, he became the first recorded motor vehicle fatality in the Western Hemisphere. This sign was erected to remember Mr. Bliss on the centennial of his untimely death and to promote safety on our streets and highways.

But if you visit Tempe, Arizona, there is no plaque marking the first pedestrian killed by an autonomous car in 2018. On the night of March 18, 2018 Elaine Herzberg was pushing her bicycle across a busy four-lane road in Tempe when an experimental car in self-drive mode failed to detect her presence and struck her head on. The car's human operator, there to be able to intervene while the cars were being tested, was documented on the car's cameras as looking down while the accident happened. Following the crash, the car's corporate operator, Uber, the company famous for merging cell-phone apps with independent driver-owned vehicles to compete with taxis, suspended their program testing driverless vehicles in Tempe, Pittsburgh, Toronto, and San Francisco.

Bliss stepping off his streetcar and Herzberg pushing her bike demonstrate the tensions between multiple modes of urban transportation where some forms become subservient to others over time. Streets used to be for walking, and then they were for driving. While cars were invented in the late 1800s, it was not until the 1920s that regulations began to be developed for pedestrians who needed to cross the street. These "jaywalking" laws were highly influenced by the automobile industry, who were eager to place the responsibility for traffic deaths on walkers rather than drivers using their cars.[1] But in the 119 years bracketed by these two deaths, there is a great deal of transportation history. And the path has been bloody, uneven, and full of twists.

On Demand City

How we move through the city has had a dramatic impact on the physical infrastructure of places and in turn the infrastructure has also played a great influence on how we move.

Three generations ago, the highway revolution allowed urban workers, mostly white, a fast paced convenient journey to the well manicured lawns and housing developments of the suburbs where the tax base could be used for their specific communities. Concomitant with this process were racially coded (and explicitly stated) covenants and redlining investment practices in which deeds and loans restricted who could rent and buy homes in what neighborhoods and produced systematic racial segregation. Describing this context, Ta-Nehisi Coates wrote in his 2014 essay The Case for Reparations "The American real-estate industry believed segregation to be a moral principle."[2]

Reading history through these highway projects has offered fodder for many critical art and education projects, including Amy Balkin's Invisible-5 and the experimental school, The University of Orange. In their project "Unearthing the Future: The Art of Reverse Archeology - I-280, Orange, N.J." The University of Orange took up this history to understand the impact the creation of a highway in their northern New Jersey town had on Black and Italian neighborhoods. In an article on this work, journalist Mark Di Ionno explains that through their research, they came to understand that "The 1956 Federal Aid Highway Act... funded 42,800 miles of interstate highways, linking major cities and turning outlying rural communities into suburbs. In many cities, highway planners took the path of least resistance —buy up the cheapest properties from the people least able to fight them."[3]

Because this newly suburban white population drove cars, they didn't rely on mass transportation services like busses or trains, and thus did not prioritize them. The total effect of these kinds of disinvestments shaped the contours of transportation and daily life in urban cores of cities like Los Angeles to Detroit and Baltimore to Houston from the 1960s through the end of the century. In the meantime cities faced fiscal crisis after crisis and throughout it all, public transit agencies struggled to keep afloat. Public transit trips dropped per capita from 115 annually in 1950 to 36 in 1970.[4]

But the story of transportation is now taking yet another turn as surplus wealth is re-injected into urban cores and with that, producing new pressures on living costs and the needs of a population of privilege. This topsy turvy cycle, often referred to as gentrification, has had profound impacts as well on the shape of how we move. It impacts which areas are deemed priorities for transportation investment, how much it costs to park a car, where there are potholes in the streets and even what it feels like to take a stroll.

In the era of Google Maps, that Baudelairean feeling of being lost in the city has faded into antiquity[5]. The influence of satellite-guided GPS mapping tools has become synonymous with the acts of walking and driving. If you find yourself in a neighborhood you've never visited, you can nevertheless find the closest restroom, gas station, police department or even hoagie. Prospective home buyers can map the surrounding amenities of restaurants, hospitals, subways and even crime statistics. And if you do get turned around, that feeling of being lost need only last a second, until your Wi-Fi or cell connection lurches you back into the map. The relationship between these mapping tools and our personal preferences not only provides useful information, but also builds aggregated data sets. Technology companies thrive on the ability to gather geo-located information, and now users offer it to them on a constant basis, often without our knowledge, with insights into where a specific person of a particular demographic background might walk, shop, drive, ride a bus, and even get lost.

The amenities-driven geo-located map of urban life is having profound effects on where people spend time and money and where they do not. This amounts to corporations calling the shots, while cities get stuck with the responsibility of planning, regulation, and management of traffic, parking, and zoning. Throughout the pandemic, the streets in one Philadelphia neighborhood have been clogged by gig worker drivers queuing at a warehouse to pick up convenient store items from a local startup—turning any available space into a shipping hub.[6] Transportation planners are having a hell of a time figuring out what to do with the changes taking place in how people and stuff in cities get around. The field of logistics, formerly compartmentalized to measure trucking and shipping speeds, has been expanded to include every facet of moving bodies and goods globally, but with special precision in cities.

Questions about transportation are not limited to the numerous ways we get from point A to B, but also how we —and the stuff we need and want—move across distances and penetrate borders. Throughout this essay, we will meet protesting taxi drivers, bike riding djs, interventionist architects, and ecologically-minded walkers. The story that ties them together is how transportation investments and technology are changing and how we are changing with them.

It should be noted that there are many tactics for artists engaging in issues related to transportation. In the last decade, there has been an institutional acceptance of art in transit as exemplified by artists residency programs with transportation authorities. Transportation for America has sponsored an Arts, Culture, and Transportation Fellowship and Smart Growth America has sponsored an Arts and Transportation Rapid Response in the context of the pandemic. Such practices are happening under the rubric of government and foundation sponsored "creative placemaking," which seek to make transportation systems more visible and highlight their overall importance. This essay takes on examples that are among the more critical and antagonistic, and are woven together with context about the policies that impede or facilitate movement from immigration to public transportation investment.

Public Transit

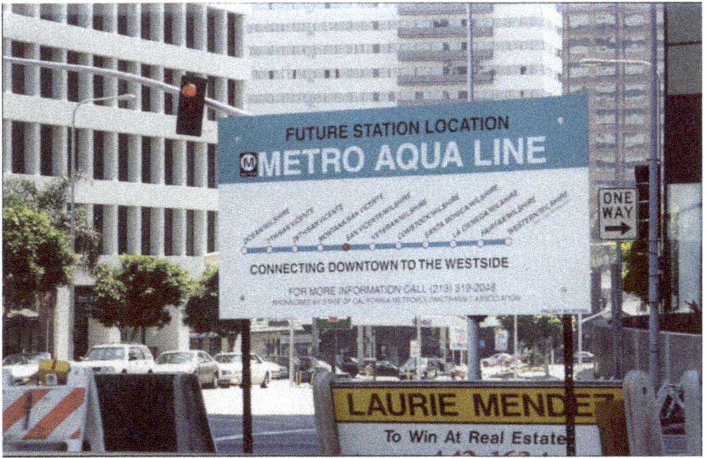

Aqua Line installation by Heavy Trash, 2000. Photo: Heavy Trash

Just blocks from the iconic ferris wheel on Santa Monica Pier, a surprising billboard sprung up promoting a new rail-line going from Downtown Los Angeles to the beach. On August 13, 2000, a group of people wearing construction vests installed eight signs promoting "Future Station Location: The Aqua Line" along a 15-mile route that advertised it would be "Connecting Downtown To the

Westside." There was no doubt about their authenticity; the signs had official city transit logos, after all.

An article in the Los Angeles Times a few days after the installation read "Signs Point to West Side Transit Mystery" and interviewed observers who debated if the new transit line would be underground or a trolley. A telling read is that one passerby thought it might be a ploy by local politicians hosting the upcoming 2000 Democratic National Convention in town to make, "visitors think we had a transit system." This guess reflected the longtime misconception by some that there is no public transportation in LA despite heavy reliance on the system by low-income, young, and disabled Angelenos traversing the city sprawl.[7] According to Metro's 2019 On Board rider survey, 66% of bus users were Latino, 15% African American, 8% White, 7% Asian/Pacific Islander, 1% Native American, and 4% identified as Other.[8]

But the signs were not official and were installed without permission by a group calling themselves Heavy Trash. In the LA Times article, the group was said not to have names attached but was described as "an anonymous organization of architects, artists, and builders who create urban art installations."[9] Fifteen years later, the high-end architecture firm Marmol Radziner took credit for the actions, explaining that their work often brought them into contact with social and policy issues they knew needed addressing but that required a different tact than their firm could officially take on.[10]

As the group wrote at the time of the guerilla installations: "Heavy Trash created this project in response to the attitudes taken by many upscale neighborhoods towards the implementation of mass-transit in their area. Homeowner groups often see mass-transit as an encroachment upon their living space by lower income residents. This 'not in my backyard' mentality has stopped many plans for the expansion of the Metro in its tracks. If the Aqua Line actually existed, it would not only serve to break down barriers between neighborhoods, but it would also benefit the environment by decreasing automotive pollution." [11]

The car famously killed downtown LA, but today the city is finally expanding its public transportation and the Metro is promising to connect downtown to the Westside, among other areas. The transit agency's website boasts its expansion's popular support with funding from Measure M, a 2016 vote to fund public transit: "With Measure M sales tax money, Metro is building a nicer, gentler Los Angeles by funding pedestrian and bike lanes in cities across the county. Our goal is to make it easier to reach transit stations, whether you're walking, biking, taking the bus, or even driving."[12]

Seen in context, this move to expand the Metro can be read as a response to efforts by city leaders and developers to re-make downtown LA as a hub for loft-living and entertainment. Such plans to reduce car emissions emerging at this moment of climate crisis is urgent and timely, as the transportation industry has recently replaced the electricity sector as the largest emitter of carbon dioxide emissions contributing to climate change according to the EPA in 2019.[13] The frustrating pattern where amenities are delivered only following significant gentrification development schemes is disheartening following the decades that transit activists like the inspiring LA Bus Riders Union, formed in 1992 to address racial and class disparities in transit, have been demanding increased transportation infrastructure and access to serve the cities working-class commuters.[14]

Back in New York, the fight over who pays for transit is a touchy subject. In recent years, a protracted fight between Governor Andrew M. Cuomo and Mayor Bill De Blasio over which jurisdiction is responsible for paying for the New York City public transit has resulted in stalled projects and notorious transit time delays. While this city-state dynamic may be full of particularities only found in New York, cities across the country are facing revenue crises resulting in changes in how people move across the city because of how taxes on gas, transit, and parking—and even speeding and traffic fines—are used to fill holes in public budgets. And as private companies jump into the transit game, how these companies are regulated has implications not only for public safety and public space, but for local and state tax income and the future of work. While public transportation helps to decrease the amount of cars on the road, there are new forces at work like the ridesharing industry, that are profiting from increased congestion.[15]

Ride-sharing

One week after his inauguration, on January 27th, 2017, President Donald Trump signed Executive Order 13769 barring travelers from seven Muslim-majority countries. The Presidential Order, titled "Protecting the Nation from Foreign Terrorist Entry into the United States" targeted citizens of Iran, Iraq, Libya, Somalia, Sudan, Syria, and Yemen from traveling to the U.S. This hit close to home for the taxi drivers in New York City with large numbers of Muslims and immigrants of Middle-Eastern descent amongst their ranks.

As swift as the legal responses began—within three days almost 50 cases were filed in federal courts—so too the airports were flooded with protestors opposing the ban. The following day at 5:55 pm, the union of New York Taxi Workers announced on Twitter: "BREAKING: NYTWA drivers call for one hour work stoppage @ JFK airport today 6 PM to 7 PM to protest #MuslimBan! #NoBanNoWall."[16]

The cellphone ride-hailing app Uber also immediately responded. They lowered prices for their drivers headed towards the JFK Airport and the protest by taxi drivers became a profit-making opportunity for this growing ride-share corporation. Activists were quick to point out how Uber was essentially crossing the striking taxi driver's picket line and thus launched the social media campaign to #DeleteUber. In yet another chain reaction, the attack on Uber became an opportunity for their main competitor, Lyft, which quickly vowed to donate $1 million to the American Civil Liberties Union, which was already fighting the ban in court. While the ride-share revolution had already placed major tensions on car traffic and the taxi industry at large, this was the moment it became an all out war that the public could witness.

The explosion of ride-hailing app usage has been great for the startups' founders and underwriters, but not for the actual drivers. In New York City, the unrestricted growth of these companies has put serious financial strain on the city's taxi drivers, and it has made it hard for Uber drivers to compete and earn a decent living. This dynamic was thrust into the spotlight recently with news that six professional drivers in the city died by suicide over a period of 12 months in 2017 and 2018, including three taxi drivers who were struggling to make ends meet.[17]

The emergence of these app-based ride-sharing tools has brought about a debate on the ethics and economics of the overall "gig" or "platform" economy, which has only intensified in the pandemic. One of the major challenges in even having a conversation about these tensions is the absence of a community of drivers—without a workplace and in their own cars—breakroom talk is a thing of the past. In response, the groups Rideshare Drivers United and London Private Hire App Based Drivers Association began using Whatsapp groups and Facebook advertisements to track down other drivers and organize actions they call "international Uber Log-OFF Strikes."[18] The group also calls for unity under a Rideshare Driver Bill of Rights, which is modeled on other groups that are unable to formally have a union due to their status as independent contractors like care workers and day laborers.[19]

Just two years after the protests against the "Muslim Ban," the same group that called for the original work stoppage, NYTWA, has worked with Uber and Lyft drivers to achieve a minimum wage of nearly $27 per hour (or $17.22 after expenses) and a temporary cap on the overall number of ride-share vehicles. As these workplace struggles continue to evolve, so do the industries on which they are based.

Certainly, a generation or two ago it could have felt even more essential to drive a car. Car companies had thoroughly occupied the imagination with movies and songs embracing the role of cars in both urban and suburban life. And while 2018 saw more trips in personal vehicles than any year on record and the pandemic has led to some uneven increases in car buying that are yet to be fully accounted for, in general today millennials and their younger Gen Z friends are driving less.[20] This has car companies scrambling to figure out what is next and yesterday's influential car lobby may today be diversifying into delivery companies powered by mapping software and subcontracted electric scooter drivers. We see GM in ride-sharing and making commitments to go electric and Toyota is investing over a billion in artificial intelligence and robotics to crack the code on self-driving vehicles.

While Uber had been testing such vehicles in various cities before the accident in Tempe and German municipalities utilizing some small driverless buses, the technology is evolving and fears of automation may outweigh reality. As one recent article in Next City magazine speculated, will these changes result in the over 150,000 registered taxi and limo drivers in New York City simply losing their jobs or will their sector be able to take advantage of the gradual shift and retrain for adjacent jobs in the new industry like "Autonomous Vehicle Fleet Manager?"

Where the rubber meets the road on the ideological divide is a concern over regulation. Next City went on to propose that driverless vehicle investments and policies should be aggressively focused in mass transit instead of those focused on individualized point-to-point transportation.[21] Failure to do so could perpetuate underfunded transit systems and access gaps for those without money, and could result in both more cars on the road and commuters riding in cars for longer distances, neither of which will help us meet ambitious decarbonization goals.

Sharing is Caring

Back in California, in San Francisco, all those internet app companies changing how people get around and communicate also have physical offices filled with workers. Those workers have houses and consumer habits and their impact on the city they inhabit has been dramatic. A city once known as the capital of the counterculture is now a living monument to the commercialization of such alternative living strategies. Curator and writer Erica Dawn Lyle reflects on a deep irony at this moment in the city's life in Streetopia, her book on art and displacement, writing that:

The use of the word 'sharing' here once again evokes the communal life of the sixties...but these small gestures, once offered for free, are now for sale… Beyond Airbnb and rideshare apps, other services offer the rental of power tools or parking spaces and the performing of small tasks. There is seemingly no area of life that does not now have a biddable price that can be set by users on the internet. [22]

One such small gesture recently seen on the streets is the rentable bike or scooter. Growing initially out of counter-culture in the mid 1960s in Amsterdam, a group of activists introduced White Bikes by collecting regular bikes, painting them white and leaving them throughout the city for people to use. While similar subcultural models existed elsewhere for bike rentals and sharing, it was not until the mid 1990s that a number of European cities began testing a more formalized system with 2013 being the year of vast growth with New York City, Chicago, and San Francisco all launching similar systems with corporate sponsorships and a huge explosion of over 65 similar programs across China.[23]

At their best, these new platforms can encourage exercise over cars and fill in gaps where public transportation is not reliable or available. At their worst, they can become an excuse not to make public transit more reliable, lead to collisions with inexperienced cyclists, and they can pile up in reckless and haphazard ways if they are not relying on a docking station to be dispensed and managed. One recent major newspaper headline read: "Fed-up locals are setting electric scooters on fire and burying them at sea."[24] In another recent case the Chinese bike-share company, Ofo, backed with venture-capital funding, literally dumped their 750 bikes on prominent street corners in St. Louis and let the city figure out the regulatory safety and financing rules.[25] When Ofo abruptly pulled out of servicing the bikes only two months after they arrived, the city was left to sort out what was left behind. While the claim was that Ofo wanted to consolidate in higher performing cities, they left the bikes behind—bikes which were in many cases, severely damaged.

Artists Matt Joynt, Anthony Romero, and Josh Rios were invited by The Luminary, a contemporary art gallery that produces the Counterpublic public exhibition every three years, to do a public project in St. Louis in the spring of 2019. They were enticed to connect their interests in community mobility to the Ofo bikes left behind in the city. The group, with members in Chicago and Boston, said that they saw the Ofo bike remnants as a monument to the failed neoliberal promise of mobility and on-demand lifestyle companies. To capture this tension between a failed monument and a community left to clean up the mess, they decided to turn one of the bikes into a mobile electric cumbia music sound cart decorated like a piñata and named "Piñata Sound System."[26]

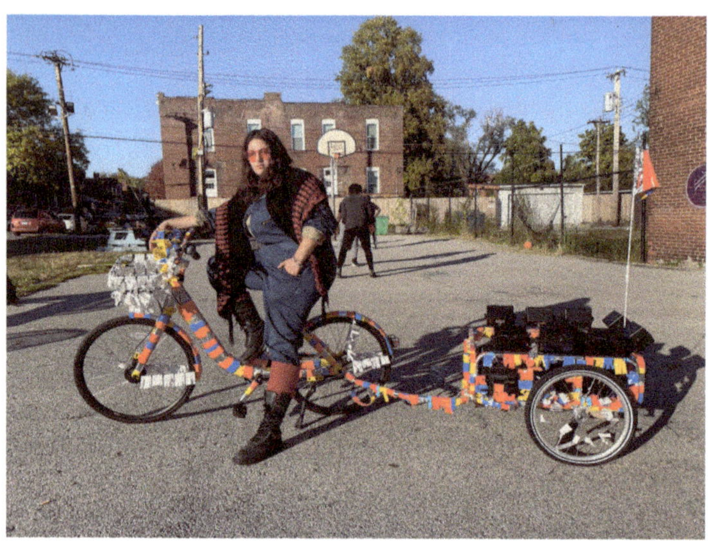

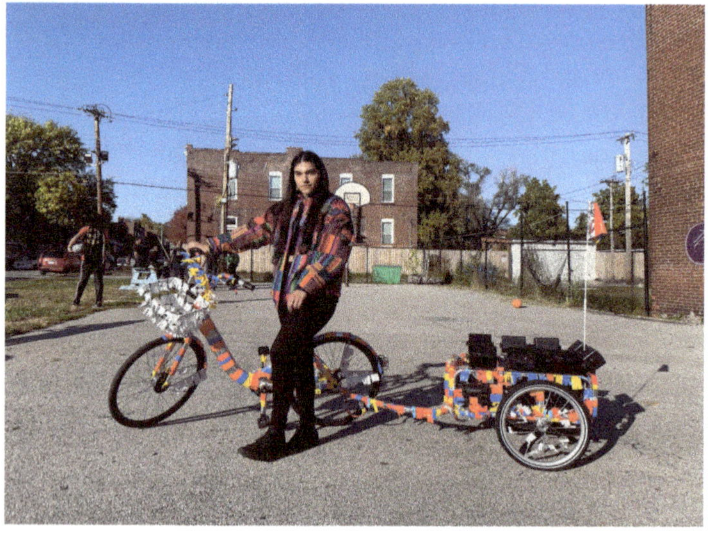

Portraits of artists Kiki Salem and Xochitl Plancarte with
the Piñata Sound System cart. Matt Joynt, Josh Rios,
and Anthony Romero, Piñata Sound System, 2019

GROUP MEMBER JOSH RIOS explained that the neighborhood they were working in is made up of Black and Brown residents and they were excited to create a soundtrack using music that has a "record of migrating sound practices that helps us think about movement and migration." He went on to explain the way the modified bike cart was able to be checked out and used on an honor system that differed from the way the "sharing economy" is premised on profit margins and a certain vision of hyper-mobile leisure and work time in the city. Rios reflected "What does it mean to create from the ashes of that object that is noisy, reflects the neighborhood, and is free? It's a revolutionary liberatory act to reclaim this gig economy object and transform it."[27]

The same "on demand" logic that normalizes using bikes and vehicles without having to deal with maintenance costs also leads to the logic that groceries, electronics, and books can and should be able to be ordered at a moment's notice and arrive within hours or days at consumer's front doors. The boom in this sector over the last year has been accompanied with a massive gap in accessibility that has major implications for community safety and deepening inequalities.

Philadelphia's food insecurity spiked with the emergence of the COVID-19 pandemic, leading many to find accessing food challenging due to changes in store hours and policies and rising food costs amidst a massive wave of layoffs and cut hours. Many populations, including the elderly and immunocompromised, were just simply unsafe in public spaces with inconsistent physical distancing measures. In the wake, grocery delivery services boomed in accordance with the parasitic nature of the gig economy. The streets have been abuzz with doubled parked drivers, becoming normalized as bikers swerve into oncoming traffic, while neighborhoods are otherwise quieter due to workplace closures and stay at home orders.

Similarly, numerous religious, social service, and activist organizations adapted to distribute meals and groceries. In one particularly tech-savvy operation, a refrigerated warehouse was staffed by unemployed workers three shifts a day to assemble boxes of donated food using a commercial delivery app designed for truckers, which allowed volunteers to then go to a neighborhood pickup site and have their deliveries sequenced for the easiest possible movement from home to home. In 2020, the logistics revolution arrived to aid mutual-aid programs.

Logistics Revolution

Before the pandemic, talk of supply chains were hidden in industry publications with names like Inbound Logistics and CSCMP's Supply Chain Quarterly. Now, it is widely discussed in tracking the complex web of relations that led to the 2020 bucatini shortage[28] and, more importantly, masks, glass vials, hand sanitizer, and other life saving PPE. But there is more to the story and how it shapes our lives and landscapes. As companies like Amazon turn the world into an assembly line, the urgency to have precise systems and time-frames connecting all aspects of the supply-chain across production and distribution become increasingly important. As labor researcher Beth Gutelius wrote:

These globally dispersed supply chains rely on logistics for the planning, management, and coordination of materials movement through the supply chain from initial suppliers to final customers (and often reverse movement as well, in the form of returns or recycling). The ability of firms to excel in logistics has become critical to competitive strategy.[29]

This "logistics revolution" led many artists toward practices of what Shannon Mattern calls "Infrastructural Tourism," which emphasize human-scale travel and movement as an embodied reaction to the unimaginable scale of the industries focused on energy, automation, and shipping—like container cargo boats and freight trains. They have turned towards exploring these sites on intimate scales through walking or through rowing a small boat through a vast chain of rivers.[30]

In this milieu, Compass, a rotating group of around 15 artists living mostly in the American Midwest, have been organizing trips and "drifts" as they call them for the last decade.[31] Later projects took a deeper dive into larger-scale industrial corridors of trade and agriculture, but always with an eye towards the radical culture and social movements countering whatever issues they might be studying. The goal of such explorations is to see these forces, which are typically hidden in plain sight. Compass member Claire Pentecost speaks of using her experience as an artist as "an organ to sense," which can recuperate what is difficult to see.[32] Such senses can be mobilized to touch and see an endless field of monoculture corn growing in a field along the highway, or to focus in on those large anonymous or generically-named logistics warehouses that line the same highway.

In one such project, Compass members Rozalinda Borcila and Brian Holmes organized a series of tours which involved physically taking walks around the perimeter of "Foreign Trade Zones" near the freight and intermodal transit infrastructure. These FTZs allow goods to be brought into a country without going through customs. As the project organizers reflect in their online catalog:

"WARNING!' reads the sign. 'This is a US Foreign-Trade Zone. Whoever maliciously enters with intent to remove therefrom any merchandise, or unlawfully removes merchandise from U.S. Customs and Border Protection control, shall be guilty of a federal crime.' These kinds of signs are usually affixed to an eight-foot high chain-link fence, complete with plenty of official-looking barbed wire. They can be found scattered across Chicago's industrial perimeter. Typically what's being guarded is a warehouse, an outdated factory or a brand-new logistics zone. To your eyes it probably looks like a dead space, with nothing happening and no one around. You're out wandering around in the Midwest, in the "heartland region," and suddenly they say you're leaving US territory. It's kind of exotic. It's kind of ridiculous. And it's probably the closest you'll ever get to globalization in your own backyard. [33]

One hot summer day, a group assembled to walk on a thematic drift called "Choking Points in the Supply Chain." The trip took the walkers to several Foreign Trade Zones, distribution centers for Walmart, a prison, and an immigrant detention center. By walking alongside and peering into these sites surrounded by fences and patterns, questions start to emerge. What are the names written on the outside of the shipping containers? Why are there no names on warehouses where they drop off and pick up? Who are the people working at the security gate? And how fast does the security get called when a crowd of people is milling about?

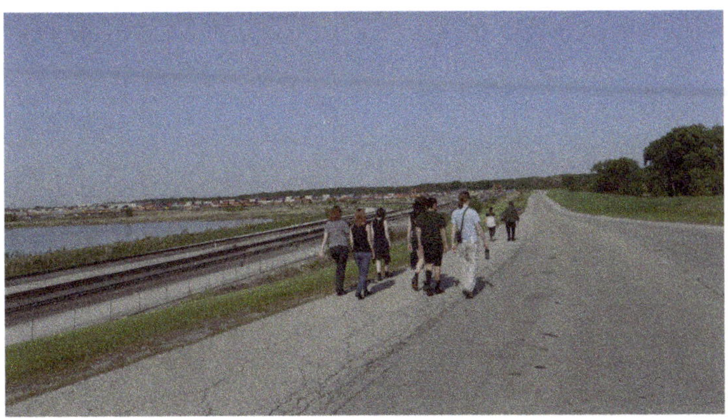

Chokepoints in the Supply Chain walking tour. 2014.
Photo courtesy of Rozalinda Borcila and Brian Holmes.

The connection between FTZ and Immigrant Detention is not immediately obvious except for the theme of borders. Describing an earlier attempt at making these connections, Borcila reflected that she has been trying to "make sense of the zone as a dynamic system, a process that integrates the mass movement of goods with the accelerated movement of territories and with the production and management of mass deportability."[34] What the process revealed is that these same unmarked warehouses often employ undocumented immigrants and that suburban counties benefitting from the existence of warehouse workers are also benefiting from the continuous occupation of beds in immigrant detention facilities in the same county. In fact, it is not a stretch to see that the same kinds of software used to track goods on a warehouse storage shelf are used to track the number of beds in a detention facility. Borcila also identified patterns of movement within the city where recent immigrants would move to the edge neighborhoods where they could live between the community of the city and the labor needs of the warehousing and logistics industry. In a piece of earlier writing, she outlines the stakes of what this work reveals:

This is producing new geographies that correspond not only to "just-in-time" production and logistics management of commodities on the global market, but also to the management of cheaper and cheaper labor and the marketization of migrant bodies.[35]

CONCLUSION

As this essay has emphasized, how we move connects us to vast and complicated systems. From the bikes we ride, to the maps we use, to the movement of goods within FTZs in Chicago, to the movement of bodies across borders, to the protests at JFK Airport and the public transit of Los Angeles, to the transformation of the taxi industry, this connection continues without any signs of stopping.

Today, artists are facing off with these emerging corporate-backed transportation tools in a number of ways, adding a third party to the tensions emerging between local city governments and the companies haphazardly product-testing on city streets.

Artists seeking to confront these forces have chosen a range of tactics including mimicking the aesthetics of power (Heavy Trash in Los Angeles), subverting new app-driven tools (the bikeshare intervention of Matt Joynt, Anthony Romero, and Josh Rios in St. Louis) and attempting to intentionally move at a different pace (Rozalinda Borcila, Brian Holmes, and Compass in the suburbs of Chicago).

The pandemic has changed much about our lives, including how we move and where we need to go. But it also simply emphasizes the inequalities and injustices already at work. Both the Trump and Obama administrations oversaw violent crackdowns on migrants at the border and in our cities, and public transportation struggles to keep pace with private ridesharing that puts more cars on the road just as the climate crisis demands we do the opposite. The ability to move has become an urgent political issue of our time.

THE AUTHOR WOULD LIKE to thank Sarah Kavage and Nato Thompson for their feedback on earlier drafts of this essay.

Land Acknowledgement

The land upon where I write this is part of the traditional territory of the Lenni-Lenape, called "Lenape-hoking." The central village of this region was Coquannock ("KOE-kwah-knock"), meaning "grove of long pine trees" and is now known as Philadelphia. The Lenape People lived in harmony with one another upon this territory for thousands of years. During the colonial era and early federal period, many were removed west and north, but some also remain among the three continuing historical tribal communities of the region: The Nanticoke Lenni-Lenape Tribal Nation; the Ramapough Lenape Nation; and the Powhatan Renape Nation. I would like to acknowledge the Lenni-Lenape as the original people of this land and their continuing relationship with their territory. I would also ask readers to consider what could be done to move beyond acknowledgement towards engagement with this way of seeing and knowing where we are. Thanks to Priscilla Bell Lamberty and Sarah Kavage for sharing this language with me on the occasion of a public program we collaborated on at Moore College of Art & Design in January 2020 and to Abby Satinsky, Anthony Romero, and Mac McFarland for sharing the ways they have approached deepening acknowledgement of ancestral lands in their contexts.

3

VISUALIZING LOSS AT THE ORIENTAL INSTITUTE MUSEUM

RAFAELA BROSNAN

As part of their 2019 centennial celebration and renovation, the Oriental Institute Museum—the museum of ancient Middle Eastern[1] art and archaeology at the University of Chicago— commissioned contemporary art installations to better show connections between the ancient world and our modern day.[2] The artists were given a significant amount of freedom to collaborate with the Oriental Institute and create works inspired by the museum's collections. The artworks include a multi-sensory installation of sculptural works *Hiraeth* and *Collateral Damage* by Mohamad Hafez, the Oriental Institute's interpreter-in-residence, at the entryway to the museum's gallery; a large-scale installation of translucent images of artifacts on the glass roof dome of a library at the University of Chicago by Ann Hamilton, entitled *aeon*; and the subject of this paper, an in-gallery installation of Michael Rakowitz's *Reappearance of Panel G-13*, a colorful recreation of an ancient relief that was destroyed by ISIS in 2015. The Oriental Institute has worked with Rakowitz in the past, but the occasion of the centennial gives us the opportunity to critically reflect on the relationship between the Oriental Institute's own history and this artwork. In conjunction with the museum's recent gallery redesign, the colorful relief brings a vibrant energy into the space.

At first glance, Rakowitz's relief reads as a creative response to the ongoing problem of cultural heritage destruction, but through the panel's tension with the other objects in the museum, a deeper impression of loss and transformation emerges. By bringing this work into a gallery of ancient pieces, the Oriental Institute Museum embraces an embodiment of displacement that destabilizes the collection while broadening its contemporary relevance.

Michael Rakowitz is a Chicago-based Iraqi-American artist who examines a variety of sociopolitical issues in his practice, and his works have taken many forms. In the contemporary art world, he is perhaps best known for his work to combat homelessness via a 1998 project called *paraSITE*, and his other projects, like *Enemy Kitchen*, which deal with U.S. and Middle Eastern relations alongside broader problems like impoverishment and hunger. Many of his pieces also reflect on his ethnic identity and questions of cultural heritage and collective memory.

The piece on display at the Oriental Institute is part of an ongoing series called *The invisible enemy should not exist* that began in 2007.[3]

Named after a processional road from ancient Babylon, the series comprises reconstructions of ancient Mesopotamian objects that have been lost, fragmented, or destroyed.

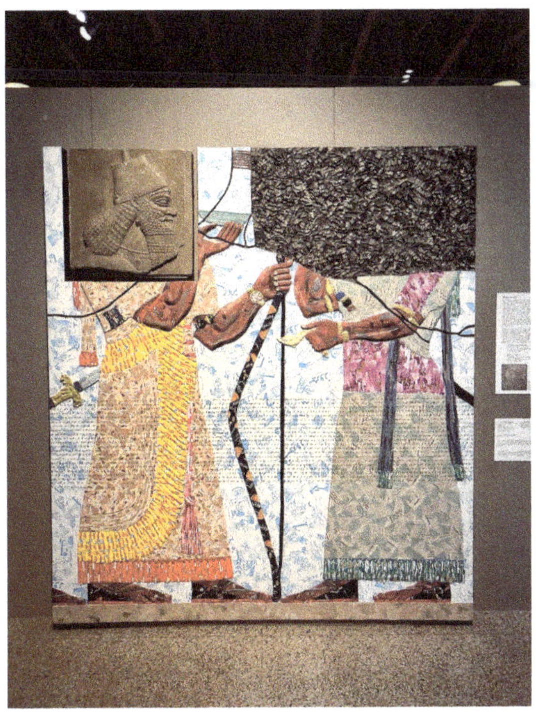

Michael Rakowitz, *The invisible enemy should not exist (Northwest Palace of Nimrud, Room G, G-13)*, 2019, Arabic newspapers, food packaging, cardboard relief sculptures on wood panel, museum labels, 7.6x7 ft, Oriental Institute Museum, Chicago, IL.

He recreates them using Arabic language food wrappers and newspapers—usually items that were imported into Arab-American communities from the Middle East. Rakowitz' series was initially incited by the looting of the National Museum of Iraq that followed the 2003 US invasion of Iraq when thousands of objects were destroyed or stolen from the museum. Many of the artifacts have been recovered, but most are still missing or at least heavily fragmented. While his series initially focused on repercussions of the 2003 invasion, his more recent works deal with objects that have been destroyed by ISIS in the past decade. *Reappearance of Panel G-13* recreates an ancient panel depicting a king facing a beardless attendant in a libation scene that was a part of the Northwest Palace at Nimrud, which ISIS destroyed in 2015.

Rather than a reproduction or reconstruction, Michael Rakowitz refers to his creations as "reappearances," minimizing his own agency in favor of acknowledging the impermanence of both his and the original objects. Rakowitz describes his works "as ghosts, as a kind of spectral presence" that can disappear and reappear in different times and places.[4] The notion that an artwork or an object can reappear is a valuable perspective that speaks to the fluidity of these objects in terms of their form, location, era, and lifespan. Furthermore, it points out the temporary and unstable nature of objects. Through juxtaposition with the ancient stones in the gallery, Rakowitz's *Reappearance* challenges the impression that the other pieces are in some way unchanging, lending the visitor and the museum an uneasy sense of fluctuation. In a very literal sense, the relief makes loss visible. While *The invisible enemy should not exist* initially began with objects taken from the Iraq Museum in 2003, many of his pieces, such as *Reappearance of Panel G-13*, focus on objects that were more recently destroyed. About a third of the looted artifacts have been recovered since he began this series, but objects destroyed through violence will never be recovered.[5] Michael Rakowitz brings back a semblance of a relief that, tragically, no longer exists. As he says, it is like a ghost.[6] In this way, it becomes an index of loss that calls attention to destruction through its brightly colored and dynamically layered materials.[7] Typically, loss is understood through absence: a fragmented object, effacement, or an empty display case. In Rakowitz's work, loss becomes an unavoidable and eye-catching presence. By displaying the *Reappearance* alongside ancient artifacts, the destruction of cultural heritage becomes a notable fixture within the gallery. Especially with regard to Syrian and Iraqi antiquities, cultural heritage destruction is an on-going disaster that draws a direct link between ancient objects and the contemporary socio-political situation in the Middle East.

The imminent loss of these artifacts makes their excavation, protection, and study especially timely and vital, elevating the Oriental Institute and its mission. Archaeological artifacts are important pieces of cultural heritage that need to be remembered, preserved, and safeguarded. To many, that type of stewardship is precisely the role of museums. The Oriental Institute leans into this interpretation, highlighting the relationship between Rakowitz's work and their own projects. Ancient Near Eastern objects can sometimes pose a challenge for issues like excavation and repatriation—they are not necessarily safe in their countries of origin. However, the original corpus he works from was stolen from a museum, the very place that was meant to keep them safe. Because Rakowitz's objects are referential to the US invasion of Iraq that triggered the looting in 2003, they implicate American institutions in this problem, causing us to ask, who is responsible for loss? And who can we trust to be responsible for these objects?

There is no simple or correct answer, and many people feel conflicted about both the removal and destruction. Here is a quote from Sheikh Khalid al-Jabbouri regarding the destruction of Nimrud, a portion of which is displayed on the object label for *Reappearance of Panel G-13*:

Maybe we Iraqis felt hurt when we saw our monuments displayed outside of Iraq. We get hurt because it's our civilization.

But when ISIS occupied our city, I felt relieved that Nimrud monuments had been transported outside of Iraq and remain protected. We are proud of them wherever they are.[8]

And:

I wasn't as devastated when they destroyed my house or when they killed some of my relatives because this is life—all of us die. But Nimrud was like a part of our family. This heritage was part of our lives, part of all of Iraq.[9]

These quotes poignantly capture the cultural significance of archaeological artifacts in the modern-day as well as the dilemmas faced by their current communities. They are not just representative of ancient worlds; they are part of contemporary cultures. And in more ways than one, the objects have been taken from them.

Rakowitz further connects his *Reappearances* to modern communities and continuing displacement through his use of materials. The Tate Modern's description of *The invisible enemy should not exist* states that the objects are "dislocated in time and space through Rakowitz's intervention," and while the Reappearances do carry a certain impermanence and fluidity, the materials situate the objects in a highly specific time period.[10] Arabic language newspapers and food wrappers that were produced in the Middle East and imported into Arab-American neighborhoods compose this relief. Called debris and detritus, these objects are indicative of the daily lives of particular communities.[11] The relief carries an added significance, more directly reflecting contemporary people and problems, and there is a direct connection between these objects and modern communities that are displaced and, sometimes, destroyed or irreversibly altered. In this way, their lives and history parallel the movement of excavated materials, which were also imported into the U.S.

Through this theme of displacement, Rakowitz explores other types of loss that are distinct from the destruction of artifacts themselves. Unlike most of the objects Rakowitz recreates, fragments of this relief still exist and are held in museums. However, these remaining fragments are separated with one being part of the Oriental Institute Museum's collection, and the other being part of the British Museum's collection. These fragments were excavated in 1846 and separated from one another in 1974 when the British Museum gifted a fragment to the Oriental Institute while the rest of the panel remained *in situ* until 2015.[12] The fragment belonging to the Oriental Institute, depicting the king's head, is incorporated into the *Reappearance of Panel G-13*, but the entire right corner of the relief, where the fragment located in the British Museum would fit, is papier-mâchéd in black and grey. According to the Oriental Institute's statements, this color marks the existence of another fragment.[13] That may be true, but the space also mourns separation of the fragments in a way. Even in what is meant to be a full reappearance of an object, we see this dark blank space. The texture makes it look effaced, and in contrast to the bright colors of the rest, this dark section visualizes the separation of the remaining fragments. By leaving the upper-right corner dark and undefined, *Reappearance* indicates that the separation in and of itself is a loss that changes the object. This move calls attention to the separation of the two fragments from not only their original context but also each other. This is true for many museum collections; ancient artifacts have been divided among museums around the world— leaving relatively few in their countries of origin—and related objects and sites have been lost through violence, disaster, or the destructive practice of archaeology.

In some ways, these types of loss are direct results of the Oriental Institute's own colonial history. The Oriental Institute is not necessarily unique in this regard: museums more generally are typically repositories of knowledge built by the colonial impulse to collect, benefitting from colonial violence and extraction.[14] An examination of the Oriental Institute's history supports these claims. The Oriental Institute Museum can trace its origins back to 1892, the founding of the Department of Semitic Languages and Literature, followed by the opening of the Haskell Oriental Museum in 1896. Egyptologist James Henry Breasted began purchasing objects for the department in the mid-1890s, largely from dealers.[15] Historically speaking, the Oriental Institute's collection is linked to the antiquities trade. To be sure, the museum's collection has been built legally, but the antiquities trade has long been intertwined with looting and the destruction of cultural heritage, especially in the 19th century.

Soon thereafter, the University of Chicago undertook its first archaeological excavations (largely funded by the Rockefeller family), bringing thousands of artifacts to the university and the museum over the decades. In 1919, the Rockefeller family formally funded the founding of the Oriental Institute, and Breasted continued purchasing artifacts for the museum, growing so rapidly that a new building was constructed for the institute and museum in 1931.[16] Breasted published a formal survey of the Oriental

Institute and its museum in 1933. In it, he describes how he views the mission of the Oriental Institute, stating "the institute is essentially an organized endeavor to recover the lost story of the rise of man."[17] He emphasizes the ancient Near East because "there still lies the evidence out of which we may recover the story of the origins...out of which European culture and eventually our own civilization came forth."[18] Breasted makes it clear that the goal of the Oriental Institute was to aid in the construction of a western narrative. To him, telling the story of the ancient Near East was to foment the story of Europe and the classical western world, presenting archaeological materials to fulfill this agenda.[19]

Now, the Oriental Institute Museum's collection primarily comprises excavated materials and just as these pieces were created, moved, and manipulated for certain purposes within the Assyrian empire, they have also been reinterpreted and redefined in modern times. Each artifact is colored by the research and displays that they have been involved in since their excavations. So much of these objects' histories have been lost to time, made inaccessible by distance and change. In removing these artifacts from their original locations, studying, and displaying them, we have both imbued them with new meanings and lost aspects of their ancient use and significance. Though excavated and accessioned for the purpose of knowledge creation, the collections of museums like the Oriental Institute are, in a sense, characterized by types of loss. Artifacts carry traces of their histories and are referential to the ancient people who made, used, and looked upon them, but through being separated from their original contexts by time and removed from their countries of origin, the museum's objects are transformed.

For visitors and researchers alike, this concept can be difficult to reconcile with, but Rakowitz's intervention in the gallery makes this sense of loss and instability visible and tangible. To any visitor, the bright colors and eye-catching texture of the reappearance will help them consider the damaged, muted, and often discolored artifacts in the gallery from a new perspective. In fact, due to its central placement, the relief calls more attention than the other objects in the gallery. The sharp contrast between the reappearance and the artifacts in both color and material creates a tension that calls the viewer's attention to issues of separation and destruction. If the visitor reads the label, the modern materials and context of destruction will help them connect the ancient artifacts to contemporary problems of cultural heritage, international relations, and simply, the fragility of ancient materials. If one thinks critically about the presence of Rakowitz's work within a museum setting, it can call into question the authority of the museum to own the artifacts surrounding it, and the reappearance makes visible the contextual loss inherent in most museum displays, especially those of excavated materials. Just as ISIS destroyed the walls of Nimrud in 2015, the Oriental Institute's excavation teams used the destructive practices of archaeology to remove myriad artifacts, from minuscule ivory plaques to colossal bull figures from the courts of Khorsabad, and brought them into this gallery. Beyond that, Rakowitz explores the different causes of loss, movement, and instability, drawing together the stories of displaced objects and communities.

Ultimately, Rakowitz's work demonstrates the ways in which the lives of displaced objects and displaced people are intertwined. Incorporating his work into the gallery space is a step toward recognizing that connection. The

Oriental Institute is not the first museum to incorporate contemporary art into its ancient galleries, and some museums, such as the University of Pennsylvania Museum of Archaeology and Anthropology and the Metropolitan Museum of Art, are even finding ways to bring groups and individuals from displaced communities into the museum.[20] Incorporating these perspectives through art and programming begins a constructive conversation through which museums can begin to reckon with their colonial histories while making a stronger effort to connect with the displaced communities who have been estranged from their cultural heritage.

Land Acknowledgment

I write from my home in Glen Ellyn, IL. At the time of settlement, this land was primarily occupied by Potawatomi villages until they were forced out by the Treaty of Chicago in 1833. The Potawatomi were virtually removed from this land by 1850. Before the Potawatomi moved into Illinois, it was home to tribes belonging to the Illinois Confederation, including the Fox, Sauk, Miami, Peoria, Kaskaskia, and Kickapoo. The Oriental Institute is in the city of Chicago, the ancestral homeland of the Council of the Three Fires: the Ojibwe, Odawa, and Potawatomi Nations, and many other tribes such as the Miami, Ho-Chunk, Menominee, Sauk, and Fox lived in this area. Today, Chicago is home to over 65,000 Indigenous people, representing 175 different tribes.

4

I MOVE AROUND TOO MUCH TO EVER REALLY BE FROM HERE

AZUBUIKE AKUNNE

I move around too much to ever really be from here,
and somehow I feel like here is close to me.
It's an upward mobility type of movement.
You know when African Americans and South Americans
moved to the North in search of opportunity.
Well it's the 21st century,
yet I'm still here looking for my North Star.
I realized life was the same no matter where I went,
came to Chicago 1st time for school,
young and wild with natty hair.
In my life and dreams, I had no care,
only a bicycle to move me around.
75th & Jeffrey to Irving Park & Kedzie and back,
the bicycle was my mode of transportation and helped me
transit around the city.
The bicycle became my business,
3 wheels and bright orange colors navigating the cityscape
selling fruits to earn enough money to escape.
Escaped with 3 comrades East to DC.
Destination: Million Man March

800 miles, we pedaled in transit
leaving and coming,
coming and going.
Emigrated from America to Nigeria to Germany to Sri
Lanka to Aotorea and many in-between.
I learned that I wasn't alone doing this transit thing.
My upward mobility began with 2 wheels,
found the uncountable
transit all moving around.
Why did I leave?
Enough time, still
I understand it's time to go again.
Older my fascination with NeuBite doesn't necessarily keep
me on a bike. Yet it keeps on the lights and helps to board
those transit flights. Yea I know one day I'll have to pick a
home,
a resting place.
That resting place might be 6 feet below the ground.
As for now, while I'm above ground
Where I am is where I am,
Where I'll go is where I'll go,
For you to see,
For me to know.

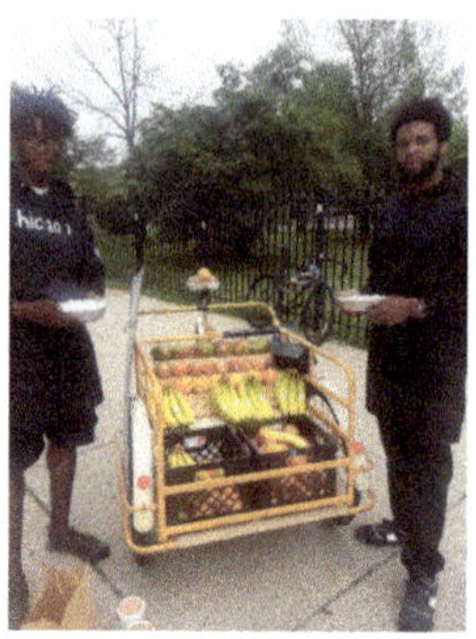

Azubuike and Chinedu Akunne operating Awo
Produce in Hyde Park (Kiikaapoi Territory)
Summer 2015

5

MISSING INTERSECTION

LARSEN HUSBY

Let me tell you about this signpost.

Chicago is made up of two grids, so far as I can tell. One is visible and the other is invisible. Maybe you know the visible one already. In this city, the streets are long and straight, and some of them seem to reach interminably towards the horizon, or the suburbs, or Indiana. Usually they meet at right angles, and usually they face the directions of the compass, so that when you stand at an intersection you may choose to go north, or south, or east, or west, but not northeast, or northwest, or southeast, or southwest. Though of course there are exceptions; there are always exceptions.

Maybe you know about the invisible grid too. Perhaps you have stood, as I have many times, on a corner nearby my studio and seen two signs reading:

s HALSTED st
800 W

and

W JACKSON BLVD
300 S

and understood that they bestow upon the intersection a set of coordinates: 300 S, 800 W. And maybe you went so far as to equate Halsted with 800 W and Jackson with 300 S, and then expanded the principal to the other streets, believing that each one is a numbered line of latitude or longitude, and that every corner has its own coordinates. Maybe then you pictured in your mind this invisible grid, floating just above the streets, a ghostly reflection rendered not in asphalt but in numbers, lines, and coordinates.

But this is not quite the case. The invisible grid is not a reflection; it is too fully realized and too pristine to be tethered to the patchy pavement of its visible counterpart. The invisible grid is perfect. Every line in its weave intersects every perpendicular at exactly the right spot to form an infallible net draped across the city. It has no exceptions.

This signpost tells one truth and one lie; or, more precisely, it refers to one place which exists and one which does not. There is no intersection of W Armitage Ave and N Austin Blvd. Go ahead and look. You won't find it; not on the ground or on the map. As far as I have been able to determine, it has never existed. It has always been one of those exceptions to the rules of the visible grid. The avenue refuses to meet the perpendicular boulevard, resulting in a hole in the pattern and a break in the logic.

The crossing of 2000 N and 6000 W, on the other hand, does exist, without question, for how could it not? The invisible grid is perfect after all, and since 2000 N and 6000 W are perpendicular to one another, they must therefore intersect at that exact right spot predicted by the pattern. That there are no physical markers at this intersection—no signposts, nor any corner to mount them on—does not mean it is not there.

Or at least I think that's so.

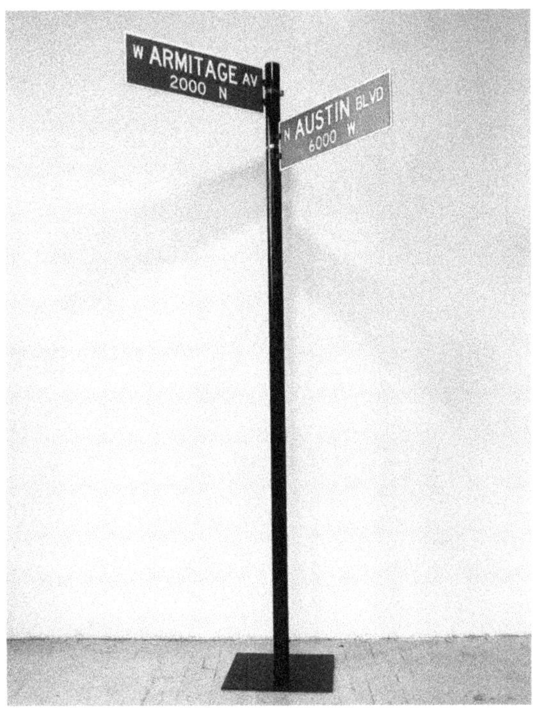

6

IN TRANSITION

ART MUSEUMS AND FRAMES OF MIGRATION IN NEW YORK CITY

MELISSA FORSTROM

Recently in New York City, there has been an increase in art exhibitions that explicitly address and represent migration[1] including immigration, forced migration, and asylum seekers/refugees.[2] Specifically, this article discusses the introduction interpretation in two of these recent exhibitions; *Syria, Then and Now: Stories from Refugees a Century Apart* (October 13, 2018- January 13, 2019), curated by Ayşin Yoltar-Yildirim and part of the New York Arab Art & Education initiative at The Brooklyn Museum of Art and *Home Is a Foreign Place: Recent Acquisitions in Context* (April 2019- March 2020)[3] curated by Sheena Wagstaff, Brinda Kumar, Meredith Brown, and others at The Metropolitan Museum- Breuer (both of which are located on Munsee Lenape land). In both exhibitions, interpretation is used as a frame to engage with these types of migration, which is interesting and unusual for art museum exhibition for two interrelated reasons. Firstly, this seems to work against the long-held belief that visitors upon entering art museums experience a universal timelessness and once crossing the museum threshold are mentally removed from concerns of their daily lives.[4] This belief about transcendent art experiences could be further promoted by the desire of exhibition creators to produce exhibitions that are separate from human concerns, desire, and conflicts.[5] The second reason is that historically, many exhibition creators are, or have been reluctant to represent contemporary socio-political issues because this surrenders any claim to museum neutrality[6] of fear of political or social repercussions[7] and has the potential to alienate funders[8] and audiences.[9] This separation and reluctance between museums and the rest of the society has begun to break down. In fact, it is believed that taking a stand on contemporary issues may become "[…] a central feature of the 21st century museum,"[10] and often exhibition creators set new social agendas that are sometimes in contrast to government policy.[11] As such, this paper argues that representations of migration are in transition from the peripheries to the center of art museum exhibition narratives which supports social responsibility in museum exhibition.[12]

Indeed, representations of migration permeate these exhibitions in the title of the exhibition, which is framed explicitly or implicitly using terminology associated with migration. This frame is reinforced in the exhibition introduction panel and solidifies migration as a fundamental theme of the exhibition. [13] However, before an analysis of these exhibition titles and introductory text, it is first essential to introduce these exhibitions.

Home Is a Foreign Place curated by Sheena Wagstaff, Brinda Kumar, Meredith Brown[14] and others at The Met Breuer (March 2016- March 2020)[15] takes its title from an artwork by the artist, Zarina, which was also on display in the exhibition. The exhibition was a group show of recent acquisitions (from Latin America, the Middle East, North Africa and South and Southeast Asia) that were juxtaposed to icons in The Met collection.

Like *Home Is a Foreign Place*, the *Syria, Then and Now: Stories from Refugees a Century Apart* exhibition title frames migration as the theme of the exhibition. Curated by Ayşin Yoltar-Yildirim, Hagop Kevorkian Associate Curator of Islamic Art and part of the New York Arab Art and Education Initiative, and initially funded by the Misk Art Institute,[16] the exhibition occupied around 1000 square feet[17] in the space that used to be the Brooklyn Museum's bookshop.[18] The exhibition revolved around representations of three different types of migration, the first story about Circassians who, through forced migration, arrived in Syria in the early twentieth century and uncovered ceramics from ancient Raqqa. Secondly, there are images of Syrian immigrants from "Little Syria" in lower Manhattan (from the late 19th century), which represents historical immigration without coercion or force. Finally, three contemporary artists—Ginane Makki Bacho, Issam Kourbaj, and Mohamad Hafez—were selected by Yoltar-Yildirim to represent contemporary forced migration from ISIS controlled areas, resulting in millions of displaced people and refugees globally.[19]

Written Interpretation and Frame Analysis

Generally, written interpretation provides museum audiences with information selected by curators and can be defined as:

The titles, words, and phrases chosen to translate a museum exhibition, theme, and/or art object that are displayed in museum spaces and that are presumably meant to make accessible and frame the meaning of the exhibition, themes and art objects to diverse museum audiences.[20]

This definition emphasizes translation and accessibility, which stresses the meanings that museum audiences create are based explicitly on a link that is established between audiences and the exhibition creators through exhibition interpretation.[21] In examining the title and introduction texts of these exhibitions, it is critical to emphasize that written interpretation in framing visitor understanding and meaning making is an understudied topic in new museology.[22] Additionally, the exhibition title and introduction panel are important because they are probably the most read and therefore influential of an exhibition. Notably, they also reveal the communication agenda of the museum and exhibition creators.[23]

Likewise, frame analysis is a multi-disciplinary research method where frames organize experience[24] and are a selective presentation of reality.[25] Relating framing to museum interpretation, art historian and museologist, Christopher Whitehead argues that frames render events meaningful.[26] Therefore, and like written interpretation, frames organize experience and create meanings from selected information. As such, frame analysis is a useful lens in understanding the messages of exhibitions.

As discussed earlier, this paper examines the exhibition title and the introductory text as frames of the exhibition.[27] The *Home Is a Foreign Place* exhibition title frames the exhibition through the distinguishing of the movement of people and possibly acknowledges the immigrant history in the United States. In an interview with Brinda Kumar and Meredith Brown, the theme of migration was representative of artist migration and art and ideas migrating as being influential in the production of art.[28] Furthermore, the introduction text[29] lists migration (amongst others) as a "culturally transformative event," which reinforces migration as a theme of the exhibition. The theme of migration and forced migration is solidified in the last line of the introduction, which reads in part "this collection display features art that explores the meanings of finding a 'home' and 'place' in our increasingly interwoven globe, whether by necessity or choice." Therefore, the frame of migration is present in both the title and reinforced introduction text.

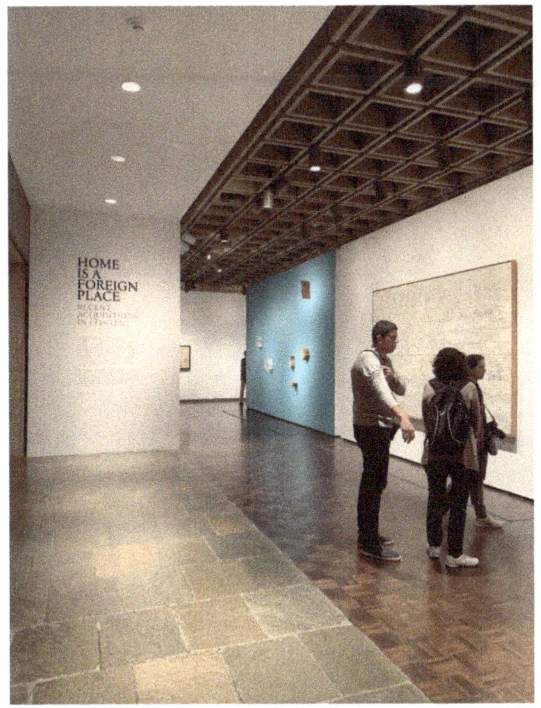

Home is a Foreign Place, Met Breuer
introduction text with exhibition entry view

Similarly, the *Syria Then and Now: Stories from Refugees a Century Apart* exhibition title references migration, through use of the term "refugees." The introduction text reinforces the exhibition narrative of migration. Separated into three columns, the text titles were "Syria," "Then," and "Now" [30] and is boldly infused with reference to contemporary socio-politics, including pro-democracy protests, ISIS, and migration. Indeed, Yoltar-Yildirim asserts, "as these changing tides of history suggest, anyone, anywhere, can become a refugee, and no geographical location can guarantee immunity." Surrounded by contemporaneity, this statement has the potential to challenge and/or transform the museum visitors' ideas and possible stigmas about refugees and asylum seekers. This powerful text engages with a contentious contemporary topic and is testament to the curator's and museums' recognition that museums are important and powerful places for framing cultural memory and opening up a cultural conversation.

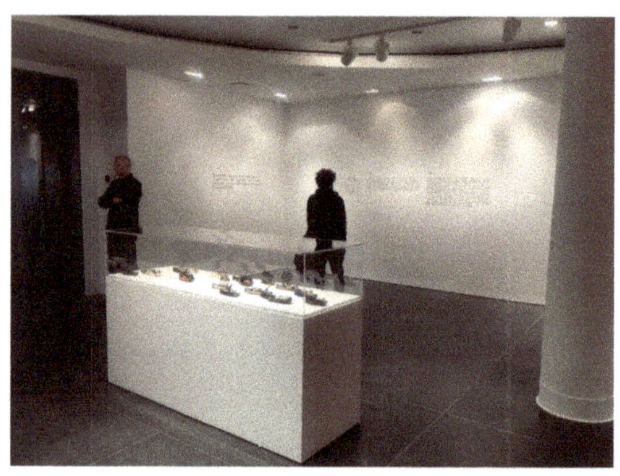

Syria Then and Now, Brooklyn Museum of Art introduction text with exhibition entry view

Museums and Migration

The importance of this framing is rooted in contemporary socio-politics in the United States and Europe, in particular, that migration has become a divisive issue.[31] At the same time, there is a growing body of research and museum practice about representations of migration in museums[32] although this research has mostly been focused on national, historical, community/local, and city museums and is not focused on art museum exhibition.[33] Furthermore, much of the academic research is focused on representations of migration in exclusively European museums. As such, this paper contributes to a growing body of research about the intersections of migration, museology, and art exhibition practice and to further these discussions in an American context. This is important, because the representation of contemporary socio-politics (such as migration) is testament to the civic purposes of the museum.[34]

In surveying art museum practice (and prior to *Home is a Foreign Place* and *Syria Then and Now* exhibitions) programs have been developed in Berlin, Oxford-UK, and in-planning at the Louvre, which employ recent immigrants or refugees to give museum tours.[35] In United States art museums, useful overviews have been provided about responses to the refugee travel ban in 2017[36] in addition to an argument in how these responses could be replicated to make museum-going relevant to contemporary audiences.[37] Moreover, there have been important art acquisitions in which migration is a theme, including "Refugee Flag" by Yara Said (2016), which was acquired by both Victoria and Albert Museum (V&A) in London and the Museum of Modern Art (MoMA)- New York. This flag was created by Said to fly at the 2016 Rio Olympics in order to enable refugees (and/or people without a nation) to compete in the Olympics. Although that didn't happen, the flag was on display in prominent areas at both the V&A and MoMA.[38] As stated earlier and with a few exceptions,[39] rarely has the theme of migration in art museums been explored generally and there has yet to be robust research undertaken in an American context. Also, both institutions—The Met and Brooklyn Museum do not have programs that involve recent immigrants or refugees.

Outside of art museum programs and acquisitions, the European Museum in an age of migrations (MeLa) project (2011-2015) explored the importance of place in European museums, in particular the intersection of place, identity, and belonging in reference to migration and the movement of people.[40] As one of numerous outputs of the MeLA project, Ruth Noack argues for a shift in the perception of audience involvement from *after* the exhibition has been created, in programs for example, to curatorial partnership that influences creative processes in the entire exhibition development process.[41] Taking this approach, Noack argues, could lead to the favoring of a migratory experience narrative over the migrant person as subject. This is ideal because it can begin to eradicate the "stereotypical and one-dimensional identities" which can ultimately reinforce an 'us' (not migrant & citizen) and 'them' (migrant & foreign) dichotomy.[42] Furthermore, the narrative of migratory experience promotes diverse narratives and has the potential to be socially transformative in that it can challenge a visitor's hackneyed understanding of migration.

Importantly, both exhibitions employ a migratory experience narrative; The *Home Is a Foreign Place* exhibition focuses on migratory experiences as an integral part of contemporary society (since the 1940s) and thus eschews the narrative of individual migrants.[43] Similarly, *Syria, Then and Now: Stories from Refugees a Century Apart* also privileges narratives about migratory experiences without a focus on individuals. In both cases this can promote diverse narratives and has the potential to be socially transformative.

Conclusion

Representations of contemporary migration are transitioning from the periphery to the center of museum exhibition narratives. In both exhibitions discussed, the title frames the exhibition through the lens of different types of migration. This is then reinforced in the introduction text, which in both cases, explicitly reference contemporary migration. Although *Home Is a Foreign Place* has probably more subtle references, it foregrounds migration as an integral part of the contemporary experience. *Syria, Then and Now* boldly frames the exhibition with three narratives of migration while explicitly linking the exhibition to contemporary socio-politics. Furthermore, both exhibitionary frames privilege narratives of migratory experience, which can transform stereotypical ways of thinking about migration. At the same time, the legacies of these exhibitions are unclear as both were temporary exhibitions and for a finite amount of time. It is likely that many migration narratives have not been translated into permanent collections, which tend to have more conservative approaches to displays.[44] Additionally, another limitation is that immigrants or migrants were not involved in the production process of either exhibition, which is established good practice in many European museums.[45] Nonetheless, each exhibition elucidated long absent/underrepresented migration narratives in art museums. Looking ahead, there is still much work to be done by curators, museum professionals and museologists, all of which can contribute to the deficit of practice and research on this multidimensional topic. As such, this article hopes to make a small contribution to this important and timely research.

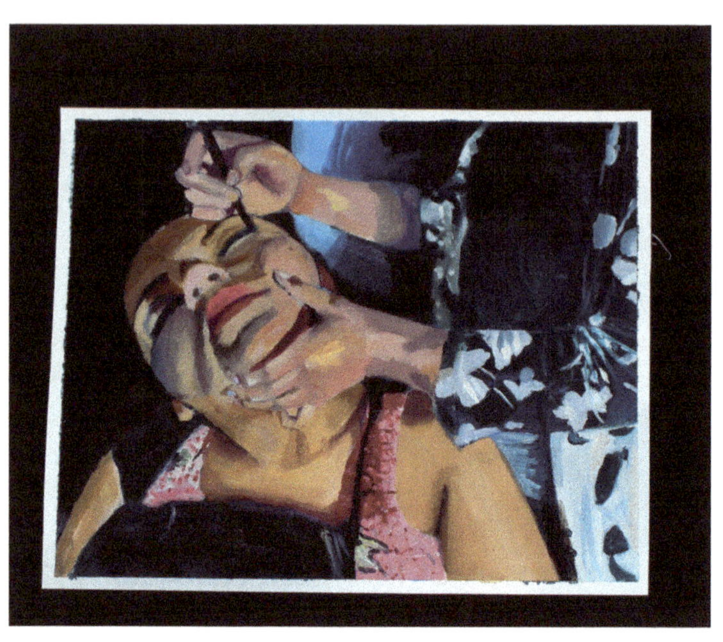

Kaelyn Andrade

El Maquillaje (The Makeover), 2018

Oil on canvas

"THIS PIECE SPEAKS MORE to the social expectations we often place on young women and more specifically during their coming of age and transition to adulthood. Young women are often pressured or convinced to wear dresses, crowns, and wear makeup to symbolize their womanhood and their femininity. What seems like a simple act, putting on makeup, dressing up, and dating can be traumatic or damaging to the development of these young women's identity and how they personally chose to represent their gender or their sexuality. El Maquillaje uses the ritual of the young woman being painted on her birthday, which is an essential part of transitioning into a woman and something that is more aggressive and shows the lack of consent that some young women experience in order to conform and continue traditions for coming of age."

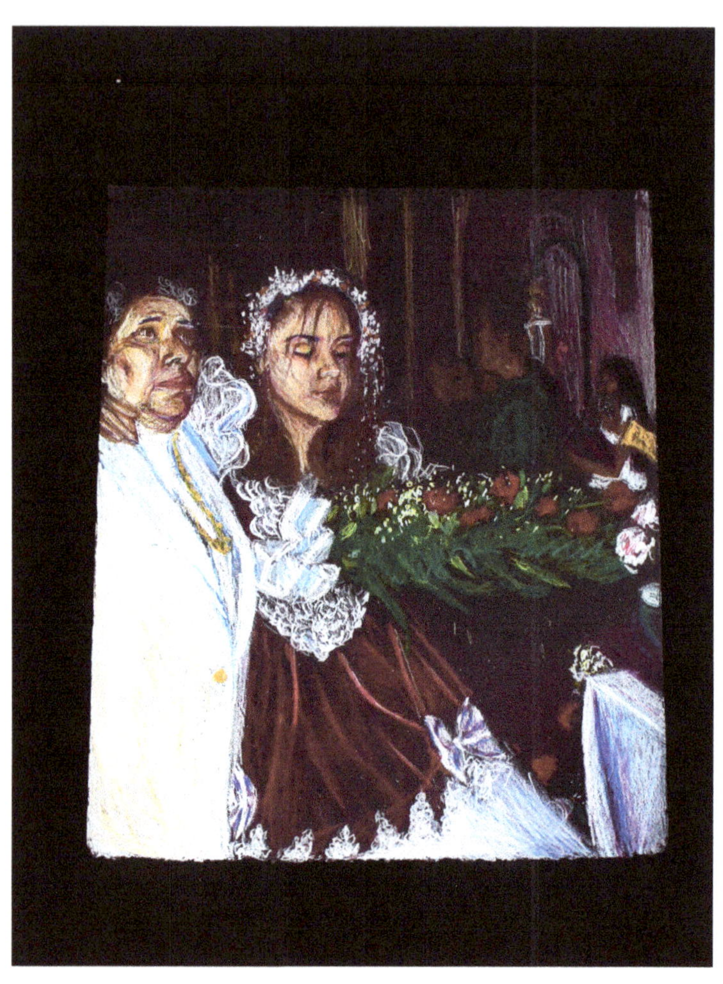

Kaelyn Andrade

Compremiso (Promise), 2018

Color pencil on black paper

"COMPREMISO SPEAKS about the religious component of quinceaneras in which young women will promise abstinence and a commitment to their faith. This represents a transition, not just that of her coming of age, but the development of her commitment to god and her family. Religious transitions and devotion is something that young women have to experience from a child to woman and then from woman to wife all under the watchful eye of god and her loved ones."

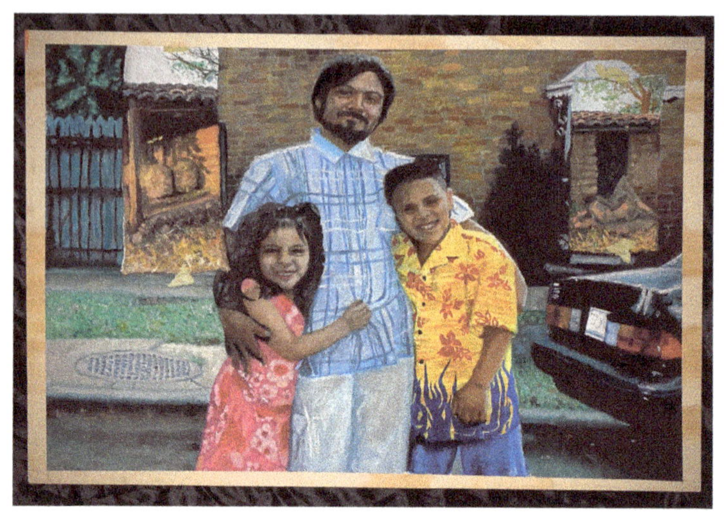

Kaelyn Andrade

Empty Homes, 2020

Oil on wood

"TRANSITION IS MANIFESTED through space and time. *Empty Homes*, shows a collage of adaptation and change. At the center, we see a man that is caught between spaces and in the process of transitioning from his home in El Salvador. The pictures are crudely pasted on his new home in Chicago while he is holding his children who are now his new home. This is the end of who he was and hopefully his escape of the in-between."

PART 2

TRANSITION

7

RESPONDING TO ACTIVISM

NEW COLLECTION, 'MUSEUMS, SEXUALITY, AND GENDER ACTIVISM,' TAKES ANOTHER LOOK AT GENDER AND SEXUALITY IN THE MUSEUM

MARGARET MIDDLETON

Museums, Sexuality, and Gender Activism is the follow-up collection to the 2010 volume *Gender, Sexuality, and Museums: A Routledge Reader,* edited by Amy K. Levin. In the new book, Joshua Adair[1] joins Levin as co-editor, and together they aim to capture developments in museum practice, case studies, and research that have emerged in the past decade, this time with an added emphasis on activism. *Museums, Sexuality, and Gender Activism* is part of Routledge's Museum Meanings series edited by Richard Sandell and Christina Kreps. The series responds to recent significant shifts in museological practice and uses interdisciplinary investigations to explore the changing role of museums. The authors of the chapters in this collection, ranging from the emerging to the established, draw on a diverse set of perspectives including theoretical, practical, and critical, and consider themes of inclusion, representation, and co-production in art and history museums.

With such a broad subject, the book does cover a lot of ground, and it comes together cohesively thanks to a strong editorial voice. Chapters frequently reference other chapters, helping build connections across case studies and concepts. Connections between queer activism and feminist activism, however, are weak and miss opportunities to recognize the lineage of gender analysis that provides the foundation for our understanding of sexuality studies and queer activism. The case studies are valuable, but as a collection, the book misses the mark when it comes to trans and queer themes and expertise.

The collection does meet its goal of grappling with contemporary issues and activism and three chapters emerge as indicators of that success. Since the publishing of the volume's predecessor, the #MuseumsAreNotNeutral campaign[2] led by LaTanya Autry and Mike Murawski has had a tremendous impact on the field, urging museum practitioners to consider their roles in upholding white supremacy. Reflective of the impact of this campaign, as well as international conversations driven by civil rights movements like Black Lives Matter, these three chapters focus on how museums interpret and interact with prisons, coloniality, and slavery. One particularly powerful chapter is "Empty, Displaced, Assimilated: Spatial Politics of Gender in Ankara Ulukanlar Prison Museum" by Özge Kelekçi and Meral Akbaş, which details the erasure of violence against women inmates at a Turkish prison that is now a museum. The authors' critique of the prison museum is uniquely poignant because of the authors' intimate experience with the site: one was a political prisoner in Ulucanlar and the other witnessed massacres and resistance efforts there. Now PhD students at Middle East Technical University in Ankara, Kelekçi and Akbaş explain how the recently museum-ified prison artificially empties and decontextualizes the place, smoothing over and omitting the gendered violence the authors witnessed firsthand.

In "'A Battlefield All Their Own': Selling Women's Fiction as Fact at Plantation Museums," Joshua Adair, associate professor of English at Murray State University, analyzes the problematic relationship between contemporary Christian romance novels and the plantations on which they are set. Specifically, Adair looks at one author's bibliography of such novels, written for white heterosexual women and set during the Civil War. The popularity of the novels has driven attendance to the plantations, which now operate as museums. In recent years, Black Lives Matter protests have demanded a national reckoning with Confederate nostalgia, spurring public debate over the role of museums in housing and interpreting Confederate symbols and memorials.[3] Plantation museums have largely welcomed the increase in ticket sales and wedding venue rentals due to the popularity of the novels, despite their historical inaccuracies. Adair notes the dangerous tropes on which the relationships between Christian romance novels and plantation museums hinge, including: antebellum nostalgia, "lost cause," and "states' rights" narratives, the master who treats slaves "like family," patriarchal romance, and the innocence of white women.

In "Kent Monkman's Shame and Prejudice: Artist Curation as Queer Decolonial Museum Practice," Ann Cvetkovich, Director of Women's and Gender Studies at Carleton University in Ottawa, describes the curatorial interventions of Cree artist Kent Monkman. The artist installs his paintings and sculptures alongside museum objects to insert indigenous narratives into the colonial space of the museum. Thanks to activist movements like Decolonize This Place,[4] calls for museums to address their colonial legacies have gained traction in some museum spheres. Monkman's approach specifically responds to the ways institutions perpetuate colonial attitudes and concepts regarding gender and sexuality. Identifying as queer, cisgender, and two-spirit, Monkman speaks through Miss Chief Eagle Testickle (a play on the words "mischief" and "egotistical"), his high-heel wearing alter-ego, a trickster character who shape-shifts and time-travels through the historical scenes Monkman recreates in his paintings as he narrates the exhibition catalog. Through Miss Chief, Monkman uses humor and eroticism to address the painful history of colonialism and genocide of indigenous people in Canada. A troubling oversight in this chapter, however, is any mention of the criticism of the artist's relationships with institutions and themes of sexual violence in his work. Two-spirit art historian and curator Regan de Loggans (Mississippi Choctaw/ Ki'Che Maya) describes Monkman as perpetuating the patriarchal privilege he benefits from and using representation and multiculturalism posed as reparations in such a way that "absolves institutions of their participation in the system of colonialism, and continues the erasure of genocide and its legacy by offering a mythology of shared pain and struggle with settlers."[5] Because of the unique cultural trauma experienced by Indigenous women, trans, and two-spirit people through sexual assault and colonial violence, they are better positioned to critique Monkman's work, even more than a scholar like Cvetovich who has written extensively about queer trauma.

The editors do address the gaps in author expertise and experience and make mention of the notion of emotional labor and the importance of compensating contributors for co-production efforts. Under current hierarchical structures in museums that reify heteronormative patterns, when marginalized people are invited to participate in their own "inclusion," sometimes by reliving their own trauma or collaborating with an institution that has wronged them,[6] there must be some incentive for their participation or attempt at reciprocity. Levin talks about how this played out in the creation of the book itself. In the introduction, she points to the absence of Black women from the list of contributors to the collection, noting that would-be contributors had requested to be paid for their work. The editors could have illuminated the breadth of representation the book does include had they asked authors to express their own positionality (race, sexuality, gender, disability status, etc.) in their chapters. Another significant shortcoming of the book is the lack of attention to trans scholarship and trans experience in the museum space. Departing from the more scholarly articles of the first four sections, the last section about trans content in museums relies heavily on interviews with trans people who do not work in the museum field. Levin et. al. also demonstrate a lack of fluency in basic trans terminology, in one instance describing a hypothetical trans man binding his chest as a "woman in transition."[7] Two authors' remarks describing queer sex acts as "uncomfortable to watch"[8] and "abhorrent"[9] betray a discomfort with the subject matter. At the same time, some chapters casually reference queer scholarship, suggesting an assumption of the reader's familiarity with queer theory. This tension makes me wonder who the editors imagine their readers to be and who this assumption neglects.

In a discipline that continues to harbor so much shame and fear around telling the stories of queer people and their histories, this book is an important contribution—but it should not be the only book of its kind on the museum professional's bookshelf. *Museums, Sexuality, and Gender Activism* will be particularly useful to anyone in curatorial or collections positions at an art or history museum who are looking for practitioners' accounts, interesting case studies, and critiques of exhibition projects that deal with gender or sexuality. The gaps in author experience and expertise in this collection reveal opportunities for future contributions. As did its forebear *Gender, Sexuality, and Museums: A Routledge Reader,* I am confident this book will provoke and inspire many important publications to come.

8

GRASPING AT RELEVANCY

EMERGING MUSEUM SCHOLARS REFLECT ON VALUE, COMMUNICATION, AND THE FUTURE OF MUSEUMS IN A POST-COVID WORLD

JESSICA JOHNSON & ZOE SILVERMAN

Author's Note: This piece was originally drafted in May 2020 in response to museum closures at the beginning of the pandemic. A postscript has been added to address recent developments.

In Spring 2020, a public university in California and all surrounding-area museums shut down halfway through the semester. As graduate students and emerging museum scholars, the authors of this essay narrate the impact of the closures on our professional and academic development and consider the broader implications of COVID-19 on the museum field. With over 20 years of combined experience in curatorial, education, and digital engagement roles, we are deeply invested in museums as sites of research, public humanities, and community well-being. We reflect on how this moment has clarified the value of museums, how the standard of communication within and outside of museums has altered, and how the Coronavirus has accelerated the paradigm shift in museums from being about objects to being for and about people.

From the Educator

At the 2017 American Alliance of Museum's Annual Meeting, Dr. Carol Ryff, a pioneer in the study of psychological well-being across the lifespan, challenged museum practitioners to partner with social scientists in order to establish empirical connections between informal learning and well-being. Heeding this call, I left a full-time museum education job for a doctoral program in the learning sciences. By Spring 2020, it became clear that my research project investigating object-handling and identity formation could put museum visitors and myself at risk.

Robust research over the past decade has demonstrated connections between arts, culture, and health, and the ongoing cascade of crises poses opportunities to amplify the vital role that museum education plays in cultivating community well-being.[1] Even as institutions have shifted to low-touch, no-touch, and distanced operations, museums are continuing to provide a lifeline for communities experiencing the grief and trauma of intersecting pandemics.[2] A growing commitment to trauma-aware education practices has sparked important conversations amongst museum educators.[3]

Before the pandemic, Elizabeth Merrit of the Center for the Future of Museums edited a special edition of *Museum* magazine, which imagined the world in 2040. The authors wrote of a future in which doctors would write medical prescriptions for museum visits, arts institutions would be staffed by therapists and social workers, and the healthcare sector would invest in museum programs to produce "measurable improvements in well-being."[4] This vision seems all the more relevant in light of COVID-19 and can only be achieved through new partnerships across the humanities and social and behavioral sciences. This insight is not new; however, in this 'code red' moment, there is increasing urgency to articulate the vital role of educators in fulfilling museums' public missions and supporting the health and healing of the communities whom they serve.[5]

From the Curator

Before COVID-19, museums had the freedom to conveniently and cavalierly ignore the prioritization of digital outreach and accessibility. A smaller museum, such as mine, had not been able to adequately maintain public access to our collection because of pandemic restrictions and a lack of relationship between our digital and physical work. The most daunting hurdle when the pandemic began was viewing digital tools as instrumental in accessing and serving the public. Our staff shifted focus from curatorial and collections care to outreach and accessibility; a modest budget, solely digital communication tools, and an already meager connection to the community served as the pandemic-battling weapons of choice. One of the first attempts at utilizing such tools was shifting the spotlight of our social media from objects to staff. Doing so took advantage of the relatability factor for which many users engage in digital communications.[6] Another attempt involved seeking out digitization grants for the first time in the museum's history. The grants were meant to substantially advance long-term projects like a virtual collection portal and newly pandemic-inspired projects like building 3D models. Currently, our staff is working to educate ourselves about the collaborative nature that can exist between the physical and digital tools at the museum's disposal. We strive to permanently integrate digital tools for organization and communication of administrative tasks, cataloguing, and public engagement. The pairing of physical and virtual assets is not an either/or partnership. Rather, it is an *and* that must be viewed accordingly.

The microcosm of simultaneously being a student and an emerging museum professional provides me a competing pandemic experience where the struggle to supply information and meet the needs of the public through my museum is met intimately with me as a student needing to consume such services. As a result of the pandemic, museums have struggled to provide access through such avenues as online portals, digitized journals, and archives. As a student, the largest negative impact was the slow reaction of museums to realize their lack of accessibility. Blockades like paywalls were already restrictive and quickly became detrimental to research by limiting access to the only resources available during a pandemic. Research was already stymied before museums took action to temporarily remove (some of) them.

A small museum's attempts at going virtual, and my struggles as a student, highlight how outreach and access should have previously been and should continue to be a key priority. While curatorial and collections management projects are halted, professionals should take the time to re-invest in virtual opportunities. Digital engagement creates a consistent and reliable path of communication between museums and the public, allowing museums to become attuned to the ever-changing needs of the public and cementing their value and relevance.[7] A multitude of free tools exist to help accomplish these changes: Facebook, Instagram, Twitter, WordPress, Trello, Sketchfab. These alterations are and will continue to be instrumental post-COVID-19. Improved communication could impact lecture attendance, gallery visitorship, relationships with schools, or awareness among researchers about collections.

The demand for public connection during and after COVID-19 will hopefully usher in the digitally realized museum on every scale. The prioritization of digital engagement may be an intimidating process, but it is a necessary one.

Joint Conclusions

Struggles resulting from COVID-19 represent a call to action for the museum field.[8] As boundary-crossers in the liminal space between research and practice, we—the Educator and the Curator—simultaneously observe the need for and demand access to museums at this moment.[9] The immediate needs of students and the public are in tension with the need for museum staff to build competency with the range of tools at their disposal, resilience in the face of rapid change, and courage to seize opportunity amidst adversity. The value of museums, constantly called into question by outsiders, is now more than ever expected to be justified.[10] All forms of basic interactions with the public have shifted and this moment highlights a timing advantage for museums. In considering the immediate and long-term needs of audiences, museums are striving to create new pathways and modalities of communication and understanding surrounding the physical and the virtual. Establishing, maintaining, and adapting connections to the community must be paramount. Museums fail their audiences and public missions when they devalue education departments and digital engagement at a time when access and equity ought to be key priorities.

The uncertainty that museums are now facing mirrors the ongoing and long-term challenges that students and emerging professionals have often faced as they struggle to survive under uncertain institutional support. Fortunately, we are agile and accustomed to uncertainty; we graduated into a global recession and have continuously worked contract jobs in a gig economy. Museums are lagging in a world that demands digital competency. Fortunately, we are digital natives; we are attuned to the languages of social media and multi-platform communication. We argue that students and emerging professionals—those with liminal status—are the best equipped to realize the rapid changes that need to take place for museums to serve our communities through COVID-19 and beyond. To think deeply about the permanent changes that will take place in the ways that visitors access, learn from, and value museums, professionals must reimagine digital engagement in service of communication and community well-being.

A catalyst moment has arrived at the intersections of accessibility, outreach, education, and digital engagement. During this transition, we must ask ourselves: What do museums add to the ecosystem of community-building and care? Are we grasping at relevancy for the sake of what we know is our contribution to society, or for ourselves and our institutions? Museums exist to serve the public; proactive steps taken during this unprecedented time have the potential to launch us into the digital world and transform the well-being of our communities in the future.

POST-SCRIPT: **From the Educator**

Museum closures haven't stopped educators from educating. From virtual school tours to online docent trainings to asynchronous maker workshops to public forums on radical inclusion and care, educators have spearheaded innovations in digital engagement across multiple platforms.[11] Since the onset of the pandemic, I have had the privilege to develop and facilitate mindful arts programs for families and students as a contractor with museums and libraries. Ongoing funding for trauma-aware professional development—especially for emerging professionals—paired with strong infrastructure for digital engagement and institutional commitments to cross-departmental and research collaborations are vital if museums wish to maximize their impact and potential to help.

Post-Script: From the Curator

The physical constraints of COVID-19 and the amplification by society of movements such as Black Lives Matter (BLM) have positively forced my small museum to engage and respond to its community. Our team wrote and proudly published its first-ever diversity statement in solidarity with BLM. Likewise, a lecture series was developed to discuss recontextualizing the biases associated with studying our museums' subject matter. Virtual and collaborative exhibits were curated by some of our emerging and most digitally literate team members. Collaboration and advice was sought by community-based groups, and our museum has found a small light to shine in the midst of the chaos of this past year.

Post-Script: Joint Conclusions

When this piece was written in Spring 2020, emerging professionals (including the authors) were frustrated with the lack of attention paid to their ability to contribute to their institutions. Part-time, contract, and frontline staff often were the first to be laid off or furloughed as a result of the COVID-19 pandemic. In the absence of institutional support, mutual aid organizations like Museum Workers Speak[12] were created by and for museum professionals to take care of their own. Although mutual aid has been a necessary stopgap measure, serious structural problems impacting equity and job security in museum labor remain. Anonymous social media accounts like @changethemuseum on Instagram,[13] grassroots organizations like Death to Museums,[14] and social media accounts associated with museum union movements are capitalizing on the affordances of digital engagement to strengthen solidarity and address pressing questions about diversity and justice. As museum workers bring insider conversations about diversity issues and their undervalued labor into the public sphere, emerging professionals have gained new spaces in which to champion the value of skills like digital engagement, which fundamentally support museums' public missions.

In addition to grassroots virtual organizing outside of formal institutions, there has been an explosion of content created and hosted by museums. Whether inspired by broader social movements like BLM or under pressure to respond to specific demands from decolonization efforts, some museums have seized this moment to turn away from the knowledge-dissemination stereotype and toward community support and service, and even self-reflection. Indeed, in February 2021, professor and curator Dan Hicks was invited by a number of California museums to speak about his new book, *The British Museums: Benin Bronzes, Colonial Violence, Cultural Restitution*, an event attended by over 400 people.[15] This cross-institutional conversation was made possible by the digital platforms on which it was held, the labor of an early-career education professional managing the technology behind the scenes, and the new regime of open and critical communication that this moment has demanded.

Communicating on digital platforms has invited community critique and engagement, solicited or otherwise. Industries with a robust digital presence, such as gaming or online sales, make it common practice to evolve with the needs and *requests* of their audiences, hence maintaining relevance. Similarly, museums have started to open themselves up to that demand to evolve, and so have begun to grasp and maintain their own relevance.

It is with cautious optimism that we acknowledge relief efforts for emerging professionals and the increasing valuation of digital engagement skills. At the AAM Virtual Annual Meeting in June 2020, Lonnie G. Bunch III said: "[W]e know that museums cannot be community centers...but they sure could be at the center of their community."[16] Even as we have become exquisitely aware of intersecting traumas at the individual and collective levels, museums have continued to be places where we make sense of our shared humanity.[17] By increasing channels of access and supporting the labor of staff who have spearheaded vital community conversations, museums create possibilities for healing and ongoing relevance.

LAND ACKNOWLEDGEMENT

UC Berkeley sits on the territory of xučyun (Huichin), the ancestral and unceded land of the Chochenyo speaking Ohlone people, the successors of the sovereign Verona Band of Alameda County. This land was and continues to be of great importance to the Muwekma Ohlone Tribe and other familial descendants of the Verona Band.

9

THE MESS OF THE CANON

A BOOK REVIEW OF ZDENKA BADOVINAC'S 'COMRADESHIP: CURATING, ART, AND POLITICS IN POST-SOCIALIST EUROPE'

IONIT BEHAR

Comradeship: Curating, Art, and Politics in Post-Socialist Europe compiles fifteen essays written by Slovenian curator, museum director, and scholar Zdenka Badovinac dating from 1998 to 2018.[1] Badovinac's writing—most of it translated from Slovenian to English for the first time—introduces compelling curatorial methodologies, aesthetics, and ethics that are worthwhile of critical consideration in Eastern Europe as they are in an international context. For someone who is not a specialist on Eastern European art like myself, this book offers an important revisionist perspective towards the relationship between art and art history. Badovinac's aim to prove that the progression of Modern Art has never been universal, but rather that artists working on the "margins" of the West—be it in Eastern Europe or in Latin America—and are working with local histories as well as with the processes of contemporary globalization is of the most significance today.

Badovinac's strategy of connecting the "local" with the "global" evades the common flattening of national differences while it challenges ideas of homogenization in the artworld and expands the definitions of museums, and what curating and exhibitions are and could be. Most notably, Badovinac calls out the Western tendency to focus on fixed identities of "otherness" and the embrace of stereotypes, a tendency that is so often showcased in contemporary large scale exhibitions. These exhibitions, like many clichés, express reductionism as well as provoke it. Badovinac challenges those points of view that imply, in general, prejudices that are both well established and conservative, which precisely annul the objectives of artistic creation or of creation in general. To avoid the repetition of the so-called master narrative from her own perspective, she proposes to implement new or unexpected curatorial tools and strategies which she identifies and expands on in each essay.[2]

There are revealing exchanges in the conversation between Badovinac and the editor of the book, J. Myers-Szupinska, which help to situate the reader in the socio-political and cultural context of Eastern Europe, especially in the aftermath of socialism. Badovinac recalls that "nobody really discussed what would follow socialism. We talked about democracy, not about capitalism."[3] The conversation fluctuates back and forth between a larger political context and Badovinac's curatorial approach; the dialectical tensions that bridge both spaces formulate arguments of a political nature that are hardly debated in the curatorial sphere.

When asked the complex question of How does politics at that large scale relate to the museum, or to daily life? she firmly responds that politics is about "consciously doing things to affect reality. Politics is not only about political parties or activism, but about how the museum responds to urgencies."[4] I wish every curator had this above line visibly written somewhere as a daily reminder. And I wonder, How will Badovinac's museum or any contemporary museum affect reality in a post-COVID-19 world? Was André Malraux prophetic—inspired by Walter Benjamin—about the "imaginary museum?"[5] Would they have anticipated this gradual transformation of the physical existence of works of art caused by digital proceedings that anticipated the closure of museums, visits to exhibitions, the revision of their collections, or the countless number of conferences and online classes that have displaced the varied materiality that are held and accumulated at institutions?

The essays in Badovinac's book are organized chronologically in five sections, but overall, Badovinac's writing reads like a succession of manifestos by embodying strong arguments within transparent ideological frameworks. She herself reflects on this position, writing that when she became director of the Moderna galerija in 1993 (after the collapse of Yugoslavia) and with its foundation, which became the central art institution of a new country, Slovenia, she found herself "in a situation in which [she] had to adopt a clear and unequivocal stance on many issues—not only because of the importance of the position [she] had assumed but also because of the nature of the moment [they] were living through."[6]

Badovinac's prolific writing cannot be understated. Considering the current demands imposed on the contemporary art curators—the over-production of exhibitions and constant travel—it is indeed admirable that she was able to dedicate time on the production of meaningful textual work. In a conversation between her and the book's editor J. Myers-Szupinska, she notes: "I would not be the same curator or museum director without writing, which demands I organize my thoughts and meditate on my work. The museum produces occasions to write, of course, but it also works the other way: writing generated the whole thinking of the museum."[7] In the Editor's Note, Myers-Szupinska echoes Badovinac's words, writing that her texts "are a form of institutional thinking and institutional building enacted close to home. There is a direct relationship between her thinking as it is organized in her writing and her organization of Moderna galerija…"[8].

Even though the essays in each section are able to stand alone, annotations providing more information would have added a more rich dimension to the matters discussed. Section one is titled "Exhibitions; History" and gathers catalogue essays Badovinac wrote for exhibitions held at Moderna galerija in Ljubljana. Here, she makes her most direct and compelling proposals. Her essay, "Form-Specific Art," written for the 2003 exhibition of the same title, challenges the selective Western history of formalist modernism: "to expose the existence of multiple modernisms, to challenge the selectivity of the Western tradition, and to examine the specificity of local contexts."[9] Even though the exhibition focused primarily on Eastern Europe, and to some extent, the Middle East, Badovinac observes that being excluded from the art historical canon is a concern shared by the non-Western world as a whole.

Badovinac recognizes that Eastern Europe shares with Latin America a past of trauma, violence, wars, dictatorship, and censorship, as well as a present desire to challenge Master Narratives of Western art. Both regions, operating on the margins of the Euro-American centric art history, must dedicate, in her view, their contemporary museums to the local contexts at the same time as they participate in the global exchange of ideas. She continues suggesting, for instance, that the contemporary art museum should be a place where we move beyond art history, and establish a new platform "from which we could see Art History from the outside."[10] In return, Badovinac calls for a meta-position that the contemporary museum and curator activities must hold. That is, a need to constantly self-reflect on its own position and re-define itself. Badovinac argues that colonialism is inseparable from "modernity," while "contemporaneity" has the potential or obligation to decolonize itself through a process of self-determination—creating new narratives.[11]

The question Who is the narrator? or in other words, Who is writing history? or Who is historicizing?, is central in Badovinac's criticism of the exhibitions she discusses. During the Cold War, Badovinac noticed that influential international critics and curators decided to ignore the art of countries under communist dictatorships with the exception of Pierre Restany and a few others.[12] How can this omission be explained? Was it just due to lack of information? Could there have been other reasons that would justify this silence? Were the artistic movements confused with exhibitions of official art or, on the contrary, as forms of opposition to those regimes? Only after the fall of the socialist regimes at the end of the twentieth century did new regions begin to be part of global conversations. Exhibitions dedicated to the art of the Balkan states, for example, were held mostly in Central Europe (the majority held in Austria and Germany).[13] Badovinac, however, pops the illusion bubble regarding these "inclusive" exhibitions, pointing to the western desire to integrate economically new markets into the European Economic Area, founded in 1994. These exhibitions, all produced in the West, often acted to promote multiculturalism and integration in the neoliberal sense promoted by the European Union.

THE FINAL ESSAY, "MY POST-CATASTROPHIC GLOSSARY," takes the form of a diary (with illustrations) written in the aftermaths of an imagined disaster that has left all museums and educational institutions of the world in ruins. In the "Destruction" entry of the diary, Badovinac writes, "These days my thoughts often drift back to Malevich… to his demand that all museums be burned to the ground. The only way the artworks they housed could be made relevant again, he said, was if they were incinerated—reduced to ashes, collected in jars, and placed in a pharmacy. Then, he allowed, contemporary artists could use them as a kind of medicine." I look forward to a future essay—perhaps titled "Destruction"—where Badovinac might write about the contemporary museum in times of unforeseen crisis such as the one we are now living in. How can we face these topics when the notions of relationships and connections have radically changed—when distance and proximity are understood differently from how they were understood before—and when galleries and museums are emptied? Considering the current situation, I wonder what Badovinac would say about "group-work" and her other proposals in these times of social isolation and distancing. What would Badovinac's self-reflexive contemporary museum look like?

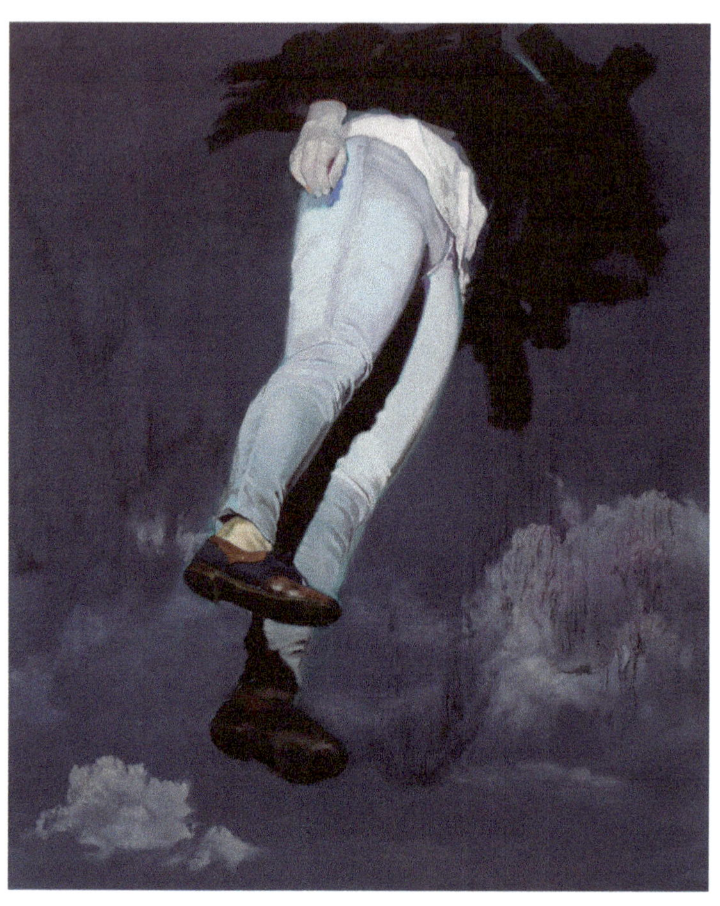

Austin Stiegemeier

Threshold, 2020

Oil on oil primed linen stretched over cradled panel, 40"x 60"

"THRESHOLD DEPICTS a human figure bisected by light and shadow in a vague and dark sky-like landscape. The figure appears to be disappearing into a type of black hole, made by an abstract expressionist-type brush mark. The title refers to the phenomenon of the body simultaneously occupying two binary and opposing spaces, and is intended to suggest a transgression of that limitation."

PART 3

TRANSFORMATION

10

PEOPLE BEHIND THE NUMBERS
INTERVIEWS WITH LAID-OFF MUSEUM WORKERS

ALEX ORFIRER MAHER, LAURA SATO, & MANON THOMPSON

Former museum workers who lost their jobs due to the COVID-19 pandemic answered the questions in this essay. We believe that it is important to feature the voices of those who have been personally impacted by the massive layoffs that occurred over the last year in this journal. Museums got hit hard during the pandemic and many had to make tough choices to remain open. But too often, they forced their staff, and specifically the most vulnerable and underpaid among them, to bear the brunt of choices they had no voice in. This journal is a space where we have power. With this power, we want to give these individuals a voice and a chance to speak for themselves as people and not as numbers. The four stories in this interview are not meant to offer a complete picture but rather to exist as testimonies of four individual experiences in museums. All four worked at Chicago-based institutions prior to being laid off, though the type of museum varies. We hope that these interviews will give you a chance to think about the people behind the numbers and the emotional impact of the choices made by those in power.

Ry Douglas

Fwd: Museums Journal: What kind of institution did you work for and what was your job there?

Ry Douglas: I worked for an interactive children's museum. I was a supervisor in guest and member services.

FM: What did the process of losing that employment look like for you?

Ry Douglas: I had multiple jobs and a freelance career, so it was really scary because I thought I had backup plans in place, but everything was falling through simultaneously and there was nowhere to go, because every museum was going through the same thing. It felt like I was constantly being strung along and had no clue what would happen next, especially because communication often felt avoided.

Fwd: Journal: How did the institution handle that process? How did that feel to you?

Ry Douglas: Mid-March, we were told the museum was closing until the end of the month. They shared that we would be paid for our scheduled hours. As April got closer and we didn't hear anything about re-opening or new schedules, they told us they'd pay us for the average number of hours we typically work for the rest of April. After then, they eventually decreased our pay. The percentage decrease was based on the bracket your salary fell in. Because our entire team was paid so low, our pay decreases were by 5%. They eventually were approved for an EPP Loan and guaranteed that we'd continue being paid until June 30. In late May or early June, we received the call from HR that we would officially be laid off as of June 30.

Fwd: Journal: On the theme of "In Transit," what are some words you would use to describe the transition out of that institution and what are some you would use to describe what you are moving towards?

Ry Douglas: It was definitely an unexpected blessing. It was the push to finally get a job outside of the museum world where I am finally making a livable pay. It was still extremely frightening though, because I had nothing to fall back on and had no clue what would happen. The words that come to mind when thinking of the transitioning out are daunting, wasteful, and pushing. When I think of what I'm moving toward, the words that come to mind are necessary, transformative, and shifting.

Fwd: Journal: If you could speak directly to your former institution, or to the field more generally, what would you say to them?

Ry Douglas: I'd tell them they need to be honest with themselves. That museum is championed for being inclusive in ways that are radical for a children's museum. In retrospect, they were just good at putting up a facade and being rewarded for putting band-aids on wounds they created or perpetuated. I'd tell them to sit with their actual relationship with the public and to think of how these interactions impact these communities beyond the museum.

Jackie Guataquira

Fwd: Journal: What kind of institution did you work for and what was your job there?

Jackie Guataquira: I worked for the Museum of Science and Industry in the Marketing and Public Relations Department as a Graphic Designer, producing print and digital materials for both internal (exhibition pamphlets, gala invitations, rotunda banners) and external (street signs, front of building banners, web advertisements) use.

Fwd: Journal: What did the process of losing that employment look like for you?

Jackie Guataquira: It was a slow process. Beginning with working from home to the eventual disintegration of the Marketing and Public Relations Department of MSI, with my position being terminated in the first round of a few layoffs over the next year.

Fwd: Journal: How did the institution handle that process? How did that feel to you?

Jackie Guataquira: The Marketing Department administration was supportive and communicative with us, and all Museum staff received weekly emails with updates on the reality of the effects the pandemic had on Museum operation.

Fwd: Journal: On the theme of "In Transit," what are some words you would use to describe the transition out of that institution?

Jackie Guataquira: Upsetting and aimless.

Fwd: Journal: And what are some you would use to describe what you are moving towards?

Jackie Guataquira: New start and pivoting.

Fwd: Journal: If you could speak directly to your former institution, or to the field more generally, what would you say to them?

Jackie Guataquira: Hopefully, there can be a slow transition into growing the team that once was.

Alkebuluan Merriweather

Fwd: Journal: What kind of institution did you work for and what was your job there?

Alkebuluan Merriweather: At the time I worked for the Pritzker Military Museum & Library as a front facing employee mainly working the main desk. My role was to keep track of guests, monitor events, keep track of sales, answer phones, and track inventory. The institution has close ties to Jennifer Pritzker who is related to current governor of Illinois, J.B Pritzker.

Fwd: Journal: What did the process of losing that employment look like for you?

Alkebuluan Merriweather: I made the decision to not return to the institution after our meeting on how the institution would move forward after being closed for a few months. Due to the pandemic, hours were significantly cut mainly meaning shifts were limited to only 3-4 shifts per week and now had been moved to 2-3 shifts per month. There was no mention of hazard pay, loss of hours, and front facing employees were expected to work in person while the majority of the staff would work from home.

Fwd: Journal: How did the institution handle that process? How did that feel to you?

Alkebuluan Merriweather: The institution appeared saddened by my decision to not return. However, at the time I was one one of the few visible front facing employees of color at the institution. I was met with "we are sorry to see you go," which I took to mean "we are sorry to lose one of our very few BIPOC employees." I had my suspicions that I was a diversity hire after I completed training, which left me feeling my role was to show that the institution was diverse.

Fwd: Journal: On the theme of "In Transit," what are some words you would use to describe the transition out of that institution and what are some you would use to describe what you are moving towards?

Alkebuluan Merriweather: Some words I would use to describe my transition out of that particular institution would be anger, disappointment, and carelessness. Summer 2020 marked the many unjust deaths of Black Americans across the United States. PMML took their time drafting a statement addressing what had occurred, and I found that to be very poor character on their part. Moving forward, a word that comes to mind that has been thrown around a lot since Summer 2020 is equity. As I continue to search for work in this field, I find that over time, many of the institutions that pride themselves on being equitable, diverse, and accessible are actually a means of creating barriers for the communities they claim they serve.

Fwd: Journal: If you could speak directly to your former institution, or to the field more generally, what would you say to them?

Alkebuluan Merriweather: If I could speak to the field in general I would state the following:

The injustice of deaths of people of color should not be a means for institutions to decide that they care about BIPOC communities. Institutions should be actively working to integrate the museum field as a means to change and not as performative activism. As the vaccine becomes readily available to the public, institutions should be striving to pay their front facing employees more, seeking to create community between activists, artists, and essential workers, and lastly advocating to answer the question, how can we move towards becoming an ethical museum/institution?

Sarita Hernández

Fwd: Journal: What kind of institution did you work for and what was your job there?

Sarita Hernández: I was the Teacher and Student Program Coordinator at the National Museum of Mexican Art in Chicago.

Fwd: Journal: What did the process of losing that employment look like for you?

Sarita Hernández: I had finally landed a full-time permanent job there after 4-5 years of contracted temporary labor. It only lasted 6 months, way shorter than any of my contract gigs there. I'm writing on my anniversary of the end of their two week notice to my termination. At the onset of the stay-at-home order, I remember our first NMMA all staff zoom meeting and feeling like this would be the last time I'd see my coworkers as coworkers. I remember sitting in my little video box listening to the silence around us when he said that there would be cuts. All the questions flooded in my head and no one was asking or saying anything. After asking the president what the timeline would be for knowing which positions would be cut, I thought, "fuck, I just singled myself out." And I was overwhelmed with anxiety the next couple days and shortly after was terminated along with other amazing queer teaching artists.

Fwd: Journal: How did the institution handle that process? How did that feel to you?

Sarita Hernández: It was heartbreaking to witness how they initially said they didn't want anyone to lose their jobs in the middle of a pandemic, and then they perpetuated that violence. All the contract workers didn't get unemployment. My terminated permanent position did, but I went many months without aid because the system is fucked and not meant for us. A year later, and I still haven't gotten those missing months of income. I had gotten by with my pies, prints, and porn. And I know many colleagues and friends that have yet to receive their unemployment. When we were terminated, we got a two week paid period to "wrap up" work. I remember thinking fuck that! I got aggressive emails from the director of education about submitting curricula, because they would have a meeting with funders within the week and all I could think about was how my coworkers and I lost our jobs and health insurance in the middle of the pandemic and how disposable I felt. I honestly felt like a failure. I didn't tell my family for weeks, because I was ashamed and I felt so disposable as QTPOC in the museum field often do. But that's the nonprofit industrial complex for you! I let myself grieve and I have to be gentle with myself for hoping that I could actually make an impact. Sometimes I still have nightmares, but I'm healing and coming back into myself and reimagining my worth.

Fwd: Journal: On the theme of "In Transit," what are some words you would use to describe the transition out of that institution and what are some you would use to describe what you are moving towards?

Sarita Hernández: Being pushed out at the onset of a pandemic was TERRIFYING and LIBERATING. I am continuing to move towards slowness and softness.

Fwd: Journal: If you could speak directly to your former institution, or to the field more generally, what would you say to them?

Sarita Hernández: Thank you for your time, but I no longer have time for your promotion of fragile masculinity. I will find and have found ways to continue my teaching artist practice and curatorial practice without you. You need to pay queer and trans folks of color more for dealing with your audacious ignorance. Stop promoting fragile masculinity to positions of power. And yes pronouns are a requirement, it doesn't matter if it makes you uncomfortable. Get with it.

If you are looking for a way to more tangibly support museum workers who have been laid off during the pandemic, please donate to the Museum Workers' Relief Fund organized by Museum Workers Speak.

11

ONLINE MUSEUMS: AN OPPORTUNITY FOR ACCESS?

LAURA SATO

As COVID-19 changes the way we move throughout the world, there has been increased attention towards accessibility within cultural spaces. As museums close to stop the spread of COVID-19, many museums have worked towards moving more of their engagement online. But even prior to the pandemic, museums had been making the shift toward online collections, exhibits, and online museum events. This is what is referred to as a 'Virtual Museum,' which is defined by web accessibility scholar, Schweibenz, as being a "means to establish access, context, and outreach by using information technology."[1] My essay aims to expand our definition of accessibility within a museum space and look at the opportunities online platforms provide to reach out to communities.

Accessibility

Accessibility is the ability to fully engage, access, and feel welcome in a space. An accessible space is created to suit the needs of many and is based on our needs as a society as a whole. In the past 50 years, there has been an effort made from various groups, including government agencies and museums, to create accessible environments and programming. Until the 1970s, museums and arts institutions sporadically considered accessibility when organizing museum environments, programming, and exhibitions that are accessible to individuals of all abilities. It was primarily due to the work of disability rights activism and the passage of legislation including the Americans with Disabilities Act of 1990 that accessibility with museums were more widely talked about. On the Americans with Disabilities Act (ADA) website, the U.S. Department of Justice emphasizes that:

> . . . accessibility enables all visitors to participate in an enriched museum experience. Investing in access - and maintaining that investment - brings museums the valued rewards of inclusive programming and a new, diverse audience.[2]

While accessibility is often treated as a necessary burden or a reactionary effort, art historian and curator, Amanda Cachia, frames access as a creative tool that can expand our world and produce new artistic, curatorial, and innovative practices, in her article, "The Politics of Creative Access: Guidelines for a Critical Dis/Ability Curatorial Practice":

> «creative access» is an important tool to deploy within a critical dis/ability curatorial practice because it elevates and complicates our rudimentary, although less important, understanding of

access in the museum. This is because «creative access» embodies both conceptual and physical possibilities, where the very idea of «access» can be discovered in an artists' work, and can be fruitfully curated into exhibitions, while at the same time, it can be incorporated into projects under the leadership and imagination of the curator. «creative access» then calls for curators to weave in a new aspect to their practice that demands a consideration for a greater diversity of bodies, represented both in the complex embodiment and consequently the objects by artists with whom they work, and also the audience themselves that visit the museum and consume their ideas. What I am suggesting is that «creative access» perhaps offers a more compelling intellectual engagement with typical notions of access: through its regular and consistent deployment, the curator, artist, and audience member will enhance their knowledge of standard conventions such as captioning, whilst also enjoying how artists engage with such conventions creatively.[3]

Cachia wants museums to rethink the ways in which they view access in museums and the ways in which they interact with access. Cachia's other scholarship emphasizes the importance of having access integrated throughout the entire process and in multiple departments in hopes that "access would no longer be an addendum to a museum budget or as an after-thought for a curator when installing an exhibit without large-print labels."[4] Museums and other institutions should be providing proactive access to the wider needs of the community and society, rather than reactive access to certain situations.

The concept of providing proactive rather than reactive access comes from the Disability Justice Movement. The Disability Justice Movement evolved from the Disability Rights Movement, an activist group that aimed to establish "civil rights for people with disabilities"[5] via the passing of the ADA. One of the main reasons for the need to change from the Disability Rights Movement to the Disability Justice Movement was the lack of acknowledgement of intersectionality. Members felt that the movement needed to acknowledge and reorient around the diversity of experiences that individuals with disabilities can have depending on intersections of race, gender, sexuality, age, immigration status, etc. Singer-Songwriter and activist, Nomy Lamm, in the article "This is Disability Justice," explains that Disability Justice is more than adding intersectionality to disability rights, it "challenges the idea that our worth as individuals has to do with our ability to perform as productive members of society"[6] and "insists that our worth is inherent and tied to the liberation of all beings."[7] Disability Justice is a "movement-building framework—a practice, not an academic theory."[8] Many activists believe strongly in a movement that is actively led by people with disabilities. An often used slogan within both the Disability Rights and Disability Justice Movement sums up the sentiment: "Nothing about us without us."[9]

Opportunities of Online Accessibility

Since art museums and cultural institutions are in a state of limbo regarding their ability to reopen their physical spaces, online programming and exhibitions widen the reach of the museum to audiences both old and new.

Social Media such as Twitter, Instagram, and YouTube, can be an excellent way for museums to both provide digital content for their audience and to directly hear from and interact with different marginalized communities. In this digital space, museums have the opportunity to get creative and to listen openly to the needs of the disability community and Disability Justice Movement activists. They have an opportunity to fulfill the slogan of "Nothing about us without us." It is not enough just to place museum events, exhibitions, and collections online. Many organizations have created manuals on ways art organizations can make their online presence more accessible. The article "How To Make Exhibitions And Art Events Accessible" by art critic and curator Emily Watlington provides links to accessibility manuals[10]. A few examples of ways that accessibility can be practiced on these numerous platforms include Closed Captioning for videos, including image descriptions within posts and embedded in images, ensuring webpages are screen-reader friendly, and more.[11]

There are many people who find museums to be physically inaccessible and/or uncomfortable places. Museums may not have easy to access restrooms or elevators, which can make people with disabilities feel unwelcome in a space. Some current accommodations, such as touch tours for people who are B/blind[12] or have visual impairments, are not currently available for safety reasons. It may be a while until immunocompromised people are safe to return to the physical museum space. Having a virtual space online creates another way of connecting with communities often forgotten or oppressed by outside forces. It is not enough just to make an online presence accessible. Museum workers also have to be proactively reaching out to people who would benefit from both letting them know that this is there and asking them what they need or want.

Conclusion

COVID-19 has forced museum institutions online and consequently placed accessibility in the forefront. While it may have been unintended, it has given art organizations and museums the opportunity to think about access. Institutions now have a better idea of what is possible online and should be encouraged to continue after the pandemic due to its ability to make museums more accessible. There is no way of ensuring that placing collections, engagement, and exhibits online will meet everyone's access needs. Accessibility allows for organizations to reach communities that have often been forgotten, but access needs for one will not always work for others. Museums should always be prepared to listen to people with disabilities and always address additional access needs. While virtual museums can be an asset to some, it can be completely inaccessible to others. Web access is not free or readily available to all people; so even if these spaces are made accessible, some people may not be able to reach these sources. In addition, many people do not have access to devices that would grant them the freedom or the ability to go online. It is important to remember that although it may not suit everyone's needs, it still significantly broadens access and should be seen as one tool of many for creating fully accessible institutions. It does not only help those who have disabilities, but also helps everyone. As we transition to a post-COVID world, museums should reflect on the vast creativity we have seen digitally during this time and take on Cachia's challenge. What can we create with accessibility at the center? Stop thinking about accessibility as a burden and start thinking of it as an opportunity.

12

TREADING WATER: SHALLOW ANALYSIS IN ADRIAN FRANKLIN'S ANTI-MUSEUM

A REVIEW OF 'ANTI-MUSEUM' BY ADRIAN FRANKLIN

LOREN WRIGHT

Adrian Franklin does not believe in the modern art museum, and who can blame him? To Franklin, art museums organize and sanitize art to death, and he is not the first to have felt this way. The titular concept of the anti-museum has existed since the late eighteenth century, although it has grown and changed over the centuries.[1] Early users of the term were opposed to the exhibition of art in museums at all, while modern anti-museums still exhibit art, but openly flout the conventions of the modern art museum. These modern outsider institutions are what Franklin has made the subject of *Anti-Museum*, which are institutions that, in Franklin's words, "successfully attempted to break down the cultural politics and civilising mission of the modern museum."[2] It is a promising concept, but ultimately these institutions—and *Anti-Museum* —fall short of their goal. While *Anti-Museum* does present a thorough and useful history of the anti-museum, it works with a shallow understanding of the museum and does not inform critically on the present moment of the museum world.

Franklin locates the modern museum's beginnings in Europe in the nineteenth century. Modern museums were first introduced to replace wilder festivals and carnivals that could not be controlled by those in power. This change effectively separated art from the people and allowed the government to govern culture.[3] These are the "cultural politics" and "civilising mission" that Franklin refers to in the introduction: the elite's control over art and culture to define taste and shape art history. It is critical that this is where and how Franklin defines the museum. He does not go back to its colonial roots, nor does he focus on its use as a tool of the state, though he seems to gesture at both. Instead, he is concerned only with the art and the public's connection to the art. This shapes how he views the modern art museum and how he defines what is wrong with it. Franklin focuses on its disdain of the public, its obsession with the art world, its focus on art history over the art itself, and its attachment to convention. Larger questions about and issues with the modern museum are left unnamed and unanswered. Every piece of museum scholarship need not contend with every issue, but *Anti-Museum* seems to gesture at these issues without committing to them.

The book consists of five case studies and features six anti-museums from the late twentieth and early twenty-first centuries. Franklin shows us how the idea of the anti-museum has progressed, presenting the case studies in order from oldest to newest: Collection de l'Art Brut, Marfa, PS1 and the New Museum, Mona, and Art42.[4] Franklin visited each of these museums himself, and he took copious notes. Each case study includes a thorough history of the institution in question, from its founding to the present day (often including a biography of its founder), and a description of Franklin's visit. Franklin considers an institution's location, labels, tours, architecture, leadership, and any other notable aspects. For example, as he is interested in how museums replaced festivals, he pays close attention to events and festivals a museum hosts or participates in. Franklin highlights how contemporary art gallery PS1 "became a hangout" in New York City due to its frequent concerts and outdoor film festival, and he draws attention to Mona's yearly midwinter festival as well.[5] He is very attentive to the humor and playfulness of an institution, which flies in opposition to conventional museums' formality. Franklin finds that these anti-museums also often share charismatic leadership, unique architecture, locations on the periphery, a lack of didacticism, and the use of darkness. After detailing the institution, Franklin assesses the success of each museum, considering visitor engagement, community relationships, and the museum's impact on the art world. The ideal anti-museum keeps its visitors more engaged in the art and for longer, has strong ties to its local community, and presents a new way to approach and enjoy art.

For any researcher, these case studies may be a fantastic resource, but they are certainly an *unbalanced* resource. While Franklin takes great pains to detail the benefits of the singular approaches of these museums, he does not consider the drawbacks. He extols the virtues of Marfa, a museum in a remote city in west Texas, for example, but neglects to comment on its accessibility. Marfa is something of an artists' museum, with great attention given to the relationship between art and its environment. Franklin is right to praise its approach, which prioritizes the proper context for each work of art.[6] But for someone who is so tuned into how art connects with the public and so against art elitism, he doesn't consider art tourism very deeply. The masses are not going to visit Marfa, which is a four-hour drive away from El Paso, the closest city of note; *art tourists* are often going to visit Marfa, and art tourists are part of the art elite. Franklin considers a location on the periphery to be a central part of the anti-museum ethos, yet he does not consider how that location may distance a museum from the public. How do museums that utilize darkness, like the Collection de l'Art Brut, maintain accessibility for those who have vision difficulties? Even when he does ask the question, he fails to follow through. In the fifth chapter, he considers whether Mona engaged a "broader demographic than conventional museums."[7] He cites a study that found that 75% of visitors were tertiary educated and only 25% were not. However, rather than focusing on that sharp difference, he highlights that regardless of education level, visitors had the same level of enjoyment and enrichment.[8] The answer to Franklin's question—does Mona have a broader visitor demographic than other museums? —is no, but he does not examine why. Just as Franklin is working from his own notes, he is working from his own perspective and biases, and while the personal approach has its benefits, it also has its pitfalls.

Franklin is a well-educated white man and that perspective is undoubtedly present in *Anti-Museum*, even if he does not name it. He does make reference to statistical data and surveys at times, but he also relies quite heavily on his own experiences and observations. Franklin is not a neutral figure, but he presents his viewpoint as neutral in this book. I respect the personal approach, but only if the author's perspective is a visible part of the work.[9] Franklin does not consider how his own position in the world affected how he experienced these institutions. His familiarity with art, his ability, and his appearance all shaped the interactions he describes throughout the book and his assessment of them. Each institution discussed in *Anti-Museum* is located in either the United States, Europe, or Australia, and was founded by a white person. While Franklin prizes the outsider perspective, he seems to mean the *white* outsider perspective. He views the inclusion of women artists and artists of color to be of some note, but not major note, even as he discusses activism in museums. His identity even affects what he himself chooses to write. In the first chapter, for example, he refers to some figures in drawings by Madame Favre as "clearly trans sexual" [sic]. The figures as he describes them are ambiguously gendered, and the term "trans sexual" is problematic and no longer in use. Franklin's biases and perspective severely limit *Anti-Museum*.

Franklin's inability to see and name his own biases reflect a larger problem with *Anti-Museum*. Franklin seems to view the modern art museum as an institution with a series of flaws that can be corrected. In the book's conclusion, he includes a table that compares the conventions of the art museum to the novel approaches of the anti-museum, as though there is a checklist. This exemplifies the largest weakness of *Anti-Museum*: it views every problem with the art museum as separate from one another, instead of acknowledging that the problem with the modern museum is the museum itself. Museums are colonial institutions, corrupt at their core. They display the spoils of war and function as powerful tools of the state to shape history in favor of those in power. This purpose cannot be removed by making superficial changes. This does not mean that these institutions and their unique approaches do not have merit, but the way in which Franklin approaches this subject matter is a bit shallow. He looks at the trees in great detail, but ultimately neglects the forest. *Anti-Museum* is therefore something of a vexing read. The case studies are engaging, and Franklin paints a vivid picture of each institution, but it leaves you wanting a bit more.

Land acknowledgement

The author writes from Chicago, Illinois, where her neighborhood rests upon the ancestral lands of the Bodéwadmiakiwen (Potawatomi), Kiikaapoi (Kickapoo), Miami, Očeti Šakówiŋ (Sioux), and Peoria peoples. She recognizes these Nations as the traditional stewards of the land and extends her respect and gratitude. Of the museums featured in *Anti-Museum*, Marfa, PS1, the New Museum, and the Museum of Old and New Art all reside on Native land.

13

PLAY HAPPENS HERE

CHILDREN AS VISITORS AND COLLABORATORS IN 'WORKING WITH YOUNG CHILDREN IN MUSEUMS'

RACHEL MURPHY-WEAST

If museums truly want to be an inclusive space for families, they need to see young children as valuable visitors who belong in their space as much as adults do. That is the argument according to the latest book from museum practitioners, Abigail Hackett, Rachel Holmes and Christina MacRae, *Working with Young Children in Museums: Weaving Theory and Practice.*[1] Their work offers museum educators a valuable collection of essays focusing on museum and cultural sites across Europe. These demonstrate how museums can welcome young children and their families, even for the most cost-conscious institutions. Published in February 2020, the book slightly preceded the novel COVID-19 pandemic. The virus has shut down museums across the world—many for good. While there may be a delay in implementing some of the book's more ambitious examples, museum educators can still enjoy this book as motivation and inspiration for what is to come. Perhaps one thing museums can take from their pandemic experience is that they are much more capable of transformative change than they may have thought. This book encourages museums to learn from the children in their spaces and embrace change with creativity and curiosity; to be open to the expansive possibilities of their own spaces rather than remain stagnant in what they have always known them to be. Those values, the essays insist, will endure longer than any setback possibly could. It is unclear when, or if, children's spaces and programs will return to "normal," but moving forward, museums may find themselves seeking new ways to make spaces inviting and accessible to families.

Working with Young Children in Museums is divided into three sections: "Thing-ness and the Power of Objects," "Museum Spaces," and "Time, New Experiences and Repeat Visits." They define young children as those under the age of five years old, ranging from infants to preschoolers. This book is heavily steeped in early childhood research and is primarily centered around theories of posthumanism. While there is no one definition of posthumanism, even amongst the creators, my best understanding is that posthumanism seeks to answer the question, What does it mean to be human? In the context of museum education, posthumanism allows practitioners to look at space and objects outside the confines of traditional language and understanding (i.e, without social construction). The sections' introductions engage in the most theory-heavy conversations of the texts, and can be overwhelming for someone not immersed in museum studies. The essays, however, do a wonderful job of "show, not tell."

For example, a central concept of part I is theorist Jane Bennett's distinction of objects versus things. The editors' musing on this posthumanist idea in part I can be slightly dizzying: "[Objects] ooze the potential to be both "object" and "thing" in that they may be legible in particular places and times, but are simultaneously rendered indescribable and indeterminate to universal sense-making."[2] Setting the ooziness aside, the editors mean that the purpose of something physical (whether an "object" or "thing") is subjective. The book's promise to weave theory and practice together ensures that their case studies bolster and exemplify their belief that young children are visitors in their own right. "The Thing-ness of Wood Chips," for instance, offers an excellent example of the practice of posthumanism.

Lisa Howarth of the North Lincolnshire Museum explains thing-ness in action. Simply put, an object serves its original purpose. An object becomes a thing when it no longer does that. Her essay illustrates children transforming wood chips, which began as objects in that their original purpose was to fill an indoor archeology dig. The children then turned them into things by using them as a tool to engage their curiosity: "Children and adults would congregate around the archeological dig and reach for the wood chips, running them through their fingers, picking them up… putting the chips down the funnel of a train or filling a metal goblet with them."[3] Young children, Haworth and her team observed, cared little for the intended purpose of an object. The concept of thing-ness allowed them to easily project their own meaning and desires onto objects. Howarth's essay, like many in the book, leaves readers with suggestions on incorporating their findings into their museum. For example, observations from Howarth's team allowed them to learn the unbridled ways children engage with museums. Since COVID-19, many museums have shifted to online learning with virtual tours and online craft sessions and storytimes. Digital platforms readily provide data analytics, and encouraging family feedback may provide insights into how people are using digital resources. In a post pandemic world, museums can maintain their interest in usership by engaging stakeholders to learn what families need to feel safe and welcomed.

Despite the practical suggestions of some of the authors, the editors make clear that this is not intended to be a how-to guide, since one's unique experience with museums is "contingent and situated."[4] This collection of case studies, they explain, encourages educators to be flexible and open to what children bring to, and get out of, museums. They stress the importance of observing and analyzing "audiences, spaces, collections, [and] priorities" for "what seems to work or not on any particular day."[5] The best feedback, they argue, does not come from online surveys. Instead, educators should regularly visit their exhibits and witness this interaction for themselves. This practice requires museums to incorporate young children's and their families' verbal and nonverbal feedback; to make experiences *with* them, not just for them.

Abstract and idealistic phrases aside, what does it mean to work alongside young children? Part II, "museum spaces," concerns itself with how children use museums. The shortest of the three sections builds on the previously-stated concept of thing-ness. Special attention is paid to "what children's bodies do in spaces."[6] To understand how children utilize museums, educators can look at physical characteristics like light, architecture, seating, and flooring. The authors of this section also emphasize the collective experiences of children playing with sound and space. These features can be applied in a playful and cost-effective way, like in the case study, "Leave Room for Learning."

Kate Noble and Nicola Wallis of the Fitzwilliam Museum describe an exploratory research project done in conjunction with a nursery in Cambridge city. They wanted to understand how young children engaged with their museum, along with the Cambridge University Botanic Garden. After describing their research process and goals, they share one of the book's most charming (and insightful) anecdotes. Titled "The revolving door: the conflict between freedom and control," they detail how the nursery group became fascinated by the mechanics and mystery of a revolving door. Noble and Wallis explain how the museum educators initially tried to keep children away from the door. After all, the weight of the door proves difficult for children to manage, and museum educators routinely keep groups away from it.[7] While the door existed to adults as a means of moving from one space to another, the young children viewed it as an enigma. The educators then turned the children's fascination into a lesson. They used the door to describe physics (the door is heavy and must be pushed) and purpose (the door lets people in and keeps out bugs). As Noble and Wallis realized, though, "the children know that they will only understand the door as an object by interacting with it and experiencing it first hand."[8] While the previous section was interested in turning objects into things, this essay demonstrates the opposite. Through explanation and experimentation, children transformed the door from an abstract concept into an object. As each child took their turn with the door, they experienced the joy of practicing agency in an institution like a museum.

While educators can look at this example and see the benefits of child-led inquiry, others can see the logistical difficulties. Group programs and tours sometimes have preset schedules. This is certainly true of large museums that, in pre-COVID-19 times, saw hundreds or thousands of visitors a day. Programs aligned with state education guidelines may also have specific projected outcomes. Similarly, many museums are now installing pre-determined walking paths for visitors as a pandemic precaution. Young children may not have the spatial freedom to engage and explore like they previously did.

Regardless of current limitations, the revolving door's enigma highlights the push and pull of educators and young children. As Noble and Wallis deftly pinpoint, "It is useful for us to acknowledge the inherent tensions between the adult's desire to teach, to shape, and to control, and the young child's need for freedom to explore with their whole being, body, and mind."[9] These goals may seem diametrically opposed at times. Educators, however, can become more attuned to young children's needs through the observations and reflections practiced in this essay. Circling back to the stated goal of part II, observations like Noble's and Wallis's allow educators to see how children use museum spaces. In turn, this encourages educators to modify aspects of programs to bring playfulness into existing programs. Seeing museum spaces through new eyes can enlighten educators on inventive ways to engage with young children.

While part II explored concepts like sound and space, part III wraps up the book with theories of time and repeat visits. It was difficult to choose one essay to highlight in this section. Perhaps the reason for this indecision lies in the realities of repeat visits. Throughout these essays, young children and their families steadily created heartwarming communities at their museums. Even in instances where educators did off-site programs, the focus on repeat visits implied that families felt welcomed by these institutions. In terms of accessibility, however, the book's essays rarely mentioned the following: racial diversity, equity, and/or representation, language barriers, and considerations for children with processing disorders such as Autism. Instead, museums focused on socio-economic divides. They approached ideas of accessibility by providing things like free bus passes to lower-income families.[10] The National Gallery of Ireland (NGI), for example, realized that requiring pre-registration for free programs inadvertently kept out lower-income families. The pre-registered spots, they found, were immediately booked by families who could likely afford a paid session. The NGI then added a "nominal fee of £5" to those sessions that allowed "the allocated budget... to be redirected to the Early Years [free] workshops for people in disadvantaged areas... as these people were typically not attending [them] on site."[11] Transporting educators directly to low-income communities allowed the museum to physically expand their reach. Even when COVID-19 is declared "over," the socio-economic divides that the pandemic exacerbated will remain. Programs like the NGI's, demonstrated their authentic interest in accessibility and equity in educational spaces to local stakeholders. These values should be front-of-mind when educators return to physical spaces and in-person learning.

One of the more unique examples of repeat visits came from Katy McCall's essay, *"Healthy Child Drop-In and Bay Stay and Play at Manchester Art Gallery."* This essay stood out because of its unique partnership between a city government and an artist. On the surface, the Manchester Art Gallery (MAG) created a weekly program where families from across Manchester could access health services from a public health provider. Looking deeper, MAG created a multilayer way to interact with various stakeholders. From a public health perspective, the goal of *Healthy Child Drop-In* was to provide "the first place where parents with well babies access health advice."[12] From a cultural arts perspective, however, artist Naomi Kendrick helped ensure MAG was "working in a much more effective and multi-disciplinary way, blending art, health, and education expertise to transform a public health service."[13] The MAG could have simply rented space to the Sure Start program and thrown in some branded pens and stickers. What they accomplished, however, transformed the MAG into a community center. Partnerships like this should be benchmarked as a model for facing the public health and social inequity crisis exacerbated by COVID-19.

Healthy Child Drop In can serve as inspiration for museums seeking to create authentic and worthwhile partnerships with their community that move beyond the superficial. According to McCall, MAG is actively more "focused on user-ship than spectatorship" under new leadership.[14] Many museums, especially majority white institutions across America, have stated their desire to 'look inward' and examine their collections, interpretation, public programs, and staff diversity and inclusion policies. This essay can hopefully motivate institutions to create lasting and impactful relationships with their community. To add to that list, McCall's essay stresses "supporting others" rather than existing "in isolation."[15] MAG did not "reinvent the wheel" for *Healthy Child Drop-in*— they provided art programs to children. Kendrick's ever-changing art installations, however, kept families occupied while waiting for their appointments. The purpose and reach of their program is what makes this essay unique and memorable.

Collaborating with like-minded organizations, even those outside the traditional scope of museum partnerships, positions museums as sincere contributors to their community.

The book often returns to ideas of community building. It is odd, then, that the book's seventeen essays rarely mention race and colonialism. Children can conceptualize race and racism from a young age, so it is remarkable that such a theory-heavy text would not solicit essays on at least one of these topics. The history museums did not mention programs that were purposefully anti-racist or dealt with "hard history." Similarly, the multitude of art galleries were not explicit in including artists of color. One of the book's most noteworthy examples of colonial and imperial institutions is the British Museum, featured in Katharine Hoare and Kate Kelland's essay, "The Sound of Little Feet at the British Museum."

Focused on their Little Feet (under 5s) program, Hoare and Kelland describe creating a sensory-friendly environment for young children. Their essay lays out how to transform potentially-intimidating spaces into imaginative worlds, like with a "Baby Tundra" full of white fabric, soft wooly mammoth toys, and bells during a lesson on the Ice Age.[16] Admiration for all things cute and cuddly aside, the conversation that loomed in my head concerned colonialism and cultural appreciation versus appropriation. In one part, for instance, the program's mascot (a teddy bear) was used at a display of Korean footwear to allow children to practice putting socks on the bear. From a practical perspective, this demonstrated that people throughout history have worn shoes and children could help the bear wear shoes too. It did make me wonder, in one of the book's few examples of a non-English history, how the museum procured those items.[17] There were other spots throughout the book, particularly at historic museums and sites, where I wondered what the full (non-white) story was, and how that was interpreted for young children. Perhaps if or when a follow-up edition of this collection is released, the editors will include perspectives of colonialism and racial diversity in young children's education.

This review would be remiss to not discuss the complexities of operating a museum during the COVID-19 pandemic. *Working with Young Children in Museums* was published in February 2020, approximately one month before museums across the world were forced to close their doors amongst lockdown orders. In July 2020, the American Alliance of Museums reported that the United States could lose one out of every three museums due to economic impacts of the pandemic.[18] Children's museums are in a particularly sticky situation. While interactives are staples of these institutions, people now view high-touch areas more cautiously. Some of this book's examples of engaging young children may not be feasible due to public health guidelines (capacity limits, social distancing, timed tickets, etc.). Interestingly, the book's final essay, Alex Thorp's "On What Grounds," provides useful models for interacting with children outside a traditional indoor space.

Thorp's essay questions how neighborhoods and outdoor architecture exist as playspaces. Working outside allowed the *On What Grounds* team to think creatively about nature, sound, and space. Throughout the twelve weeks of sessions, partnering artist Bahbak Hashemi-Nezhad often brought the children found materials, ones "with no fixed function."[19] Play, often a cornerstone of children's spaces, can exist anywhere. Museums strapped for resources can host stations with cardboard boxes on outdoor green spaces. Educators can take students on a socially-distant walking tour of their building's architecture, with movement activities or stories at every stop. Free play can occur in roped-off sidewalk areas. Some of this book's most repeated advice—think creatively, work collaboratively, center playfulness—can be scaled to a variety of circumstances. The book does not address a "what if" scenario for a global pandemic; however, it does reassure educators that their work is meaningful to childhood development. Children do not require expensive installations to begin learning. In a post-pandemic world, educators should keep their work in perspective and remember to have fun with their job.

Working with Young Children in Museums champions the symbiotic relationship between young children, their families, and museums. Essays lay out how children learn from museums, and museums learn from children. The latter part can be broken down into a practical and spatial understanding. Firstly, essays illustrate how museums have adapted to children's needs, such as creating spaces to park strollers or eliminating barriers that prevented low-income families from repeat visits. Secondly, essays demonstrate how children's presences transformed institutions into playgrounds. As COVID-19 forces educators to reconstruct what in-person and virtual programming looks like, this book provides plenty of examples to help reimagine children's presence in museums. Young children and their families can encourage staff to be curious, to never forget the wonder of visiting a museum for the first time. Children should be seen as a valuable member of the museum team, even if they forget to refill the breakroom coffee pot.

14

DEBUNK, DECENTER, AND DIVERSIFY

USING THEMATIC REINTERPRETATION TO REVITALIZE MUSEUM TOURS

DANIEL P. GRAHAM

Museum professionals have long acknowledged that museums and historic sites are among the most trusted sources for information about the past.[1] However, small museums struggle to attract new visitors, cultivate repeat visitation, and connect their historical topics to contemporary audiences. Despite the public trust in museums, interpretation is also frequently a forum in which inaccurate or exclusionary narratives are reproduced uncritically, which has become more apparent in this historic moment of reckoning with systemic inequities. In my role as the Coordinator of Education and Outreach at the College Park Aviation Museum in College Park, Maryland, I have been confronted with the realization that our museum's narrative was inaccurate, exclusionary, and did little to resonate with our visitors. However, my team and I have also identified a path forward for our site, which I believe will prove instructive for others working at small museums.

We built our tour primarily around the Wright Brothers and their successful innovations in aviation. We began the tour by discussing how Wilbur and Orville developed and tested the various components of their aircraft. Through their brilliance, the Wrights were able to create an unprecedented machine. After testing their first plane at Kitty Hawk, and receiving government backing, the Wrights began working at Fort Meyer, in Virginia. However, following a flight accident, which killed Army Lieutenant Thomas Selfridge, and wanting a work environment with more privacy, the Wrights went to College Park. There, they established a new airfield, workshop, and, in 1909, the first army aviation school. The tour then shifts to a series of historic firsts that took place at the College Park Airport since the Wright Brothers. Airmail was inaugurated in 1918 with mail delivery flights departing College Park for New York, and one of the earliest helicopter prototypes, the Berliner Helicopter No. 5, was tested on the airfield in 1924. We highlight each of these events through our historic aircraft and guide our audiences to reflect on how each subsequent aircraft builds on the accomplishments of the Wrights in different ways. Our museum's tour and exhibit interpretation has followed this narrative for the past 15 years at least.

Following our site's temporary closure due to COVID-19, my team and I launched a research initiative intended to bolster our current tour interpretation. What we discovered, instead, were several interpretive inaccuracies, inconsistencies, and omissions. In recognizing these issues in our museum's interpretation, my team and I embarked on a research-based reinterpretation of our tour narrative. Recognizing that my museum's problems are not unique, what follows is a brief outline of the scope of the problem, a description of the solution suggested by our research, and an overview of our process of reinterpretation.

The Problem

Many small museums present the story of a person or a small group of closely linked people, and something about the importance or significance of a particular site. Although we recognize this pattern more immediately in historic house museums, it is common to other small museums.[2] Through an intentional focus on specific people and places, interpretation at these museums is custom-built, fitted to those figures and sites. Although this seems obvious, and like the most natural approach to such an interpretive task, it presents several structural problems.

Through such a narrowly focused interpretation, we can easily arrive at an interpretive narrative that largely ignores the failures and shortcomings of its subject, that is consciously and retroactively shaped by that subject themselves, and that is anachronistically informed by modern popular conceptions. For example, our research revealed that far from being unprecedented, the Wrights' drew many elements of their aircraft designs from an international community of aviation pioneers, and their original contribution was combining these preexisting elements, not creating any of them.[3] The Wrights wrote accounts of their own originality and success, and years after their successful implementation they were likely influenced by ongoing patent litigation in which they had financial stakes in representing their inventions as entirely original.[4] It was largely upon these biased sources that our museum based its interpretation and tours.

Beyond the problems of bespoke interpretation, an exclusionary focus on specific historical figures largely whitewashes the past, particularly in instances where the contributions and activities of women and people of color were poorly documented in their own time. In this way, it is entirely possible for a museum which has no colonial arti-facts in its collection to nevertheless adopt coloniality in its perspective. The act of recording, displaying, or promoting a historical narrative is a function of structures of power and social capital. When a historical narrative only includes white male figures, it should draw critical scrutiny to determine if that focus is true of the events of the past, or if it is instead a function of our attempt to recreate that past. Interpretation at the College Park Aviation Museum had a conspicuous absence of non-white historical actors. The previous justification for this has been that there are no records of Black pilots flying at our site during the period of our interpretation, from 1909 to 1959. Although this is true, the lack of representation in our site's history is itself significant, as Black pilots were not allowed to train or fly at the airport. The segregation of airfields inspired a group of aspiring pilots to establish their own airfield, the Columbia Air Center, and create a flying club, the Cloud Club. Although our museum did previously have some displays related to this site and organization, there is no mention of racism or segregation in those exhibit panels, and we did not include any of that information in our tour scripts.

But small museums already have enough to worry about, right? Concerns over funding, visitation, and relevance have only become more pressing in the COVID-19 pandemic. By virtue of being small, small museums frequently rely on their local communities for support and visitation either because their topic is of local interest or simply because they lack the notoriety and draw of larger national museums. [5] How are small museums to remain economically viable and connect contemporary audiences with the past? Concerns about survival may take precedence in our minds over desires to make museums diverse, representative, and accessible, or to decenter whiteness in our collections and interpretation. However, small museums do not have to choose between addressing inequity and inaccuracy in their interpretation and increasing their relevance and connection to their visitors. Indeed, without any added cost, it is possible to make interpretation more relatable, accurate, and diverse, while decentering exclusionary narratives rooted in a legacy of racism and colonialism, all by simply reorienting our thinking, reimagining our interpretation, and reframing our stories.

The Plan

Many small museums have undertaken major initiatives to combat the issues outlined above. Each site has reimagined itself in some way specific to its history and mission. Lincoln's Cottage reinvented itself as a museum of ideas.[6] The Jane Addams Hull-House Museum rebuilt its interpretation around the idea of activism.[7] The Weeksville Heritage Center has reinterpreted its past through the lens of activism and the many meanings of freedom.[8] Thomas Jefferson's Monticello has confronted its history of slavery by creating interpretation around the paradox of a slave-owner advocating liberty.[9] Each of these reinterpretations has been successful, and each narrative's reframing around abstract concepts are relevant to the historical content, but continue to hold meaning and significance for contemporary audiences.

In *Anarchist's Guide to Historic House Museums*, Franklin Vagnone and Deborah Ryan argue that historic house museums should begin their interpretive plan by engaging with their neighboring community to discern what topics are relevant and meaningful to that community. By doing so, a museum staff can identify abstract themes which connect their community and their museum's content, and build interpretation and programming around concepts which they already know will resonate with the local community.[10] Ron Potvin cites the Lower East Side Tenement Museum as an exemplar, explaining that it "focuses on difficult and complex issues involving immigration and assimilation" using objects "to illustrate stories of real people and families" through which museum visitors "seek personal relevance, and often find emotional connections."[11] It is this emotional connection that we should harness.

Although small museums struggle to connect the past to the public in some ways, public interest in historically inspired media remains strong. Benjamin Filene argues that these media are "outsider histories," which is to say histories created outside of museums or academia, and that they remain popular because they create emotional resonance and connection to which the public responds.[12] Roy Rosenzweig and David Thelen corroborate this, and identified that many visitors connect with the historical content of museums through the emotional cues of interpreters, emotional resonance of objects, and emotional investment in the experiences of historical figures.[13] By building interpretation around abstract themes, we can create space for previously ignored narratives so that we can acknowledge the diversity of perspectives on events in the past. By selecting abstract themes which are universal and relatable, we can guide our audiences to empathize with the past, creating an emotional connection.

The Process

Beginning with broad research, both in our collections and library, our team identified important narratives which were either underrepresented or absent from our exhibits and tours. These included the stories of early aviation pioneers who were instrumental to the successes of the Wright Brothers. The stories of Black aviators in Maryland responding to segregation by creating their own opportunities despite systemic barriers to those efforts, including the creation of the Cloud Club and the Columbia Air Center (on the present day site of the Patuxent River Park in Upper Marlboro, MD). The story of women fighting for inclusion in aviation, most notably to our site through the Women Airforce Service Pilots (WASP) program and women's inclusion in Civilian Pilot Training Programs, under which many female pilots received training at the College Park Airport.

We next identified overarching abstract themes to which we could connect these new narratives, as well as our existing storyline of the Wright Brothers' achievements. After much deliberation, my team identified perseverance and risk-taking as overarching themes. Invention and innovation, like that in which the Wright Brothers participated with other aviation pioneers, requires perseverance, and entails significant risk. Creating new opportunities in the face of systemic oppression while simultaneously advocating for equal treatment, as members of the Cloud Club and early WASP pilots did, requires even greater perseverance, and entails even more significant risk. Simply reorienting a story about the Wrights to a story about perseverance created space in which we have already begun to share previously overlooked histories.

I would be remiss if I did not clarify that we have yet to see the impact of our reinterpretation efforts. Due to the ongoing pandemic, our museum remains closed, so we cannot observe or evaluate our guests' reactions to this new thematic approach to our historical narratives. Although we cannot yet measure the effect of the thematic reinterpretation we have undertaken, I side with Socrates, as portrayed by Plato, in "that we shall be better and braver and less helpless if we think that we ought to enquire, than we should have been if we indulged in the idle fancy that there was no knowing and no use in seeking to know what we do not know."[14] The precise measurement of our outcome may come later, but we are presenting histories which are more diverse, more representative of our community, and more accurate to the past as it actually occurred. By presenting these narratives through the lens of an abstract and universally relatable concept, we also create a stronger opportunity for our visitors to find emotional resonance with the past.

This has also served as a much-needed reminder to myself and my team that although we may think of history as settled and sure, it is not. Our interpretation is contingent, incomplete, and in constant need of reexamination, and it should be presented as such. Although this may seem to undermine the authority of museums, we must remember that "the goal is not to educate visitors to a singular point of view but to create an informed public—people who can analyze, criticize, understand, and manipulate history and culture to inform their lives and aid them in addressing the issues, problems, and normal dilemmas of life."[15] Interpretive plans, particularly those of small museums, can easily fall into rose-tinted inaccuracies, an exclusionary focus, and narratives which are too specific or thing-oriented to be relevant to a broader audience. If you, like me, find yourself working at a small museum with limited resources and funding, but are provoked to action by the social inequities made manifest in issues of interpretation, then I urge you to reinterpret your tour programs along thematic lines. The only investment needed to bring our ambitious project of reinterpretation to fruition was the time and creativity of motivated people. The process was easier than expected and filled with engaging conversation and illuminating research discoveries. I am confident that if you embrace the constant transition inherent to our understanding of the past, it will improve your interpretation, your connection to your visitors, and their passion for the past.

Land Acknowledgement

As an educator and historian dedicated to equity, confronting the truth of the past, and acknowledging our complicity in the legacies of colonialism, the author would like to recognize that the College Park Aviation Museum occupies land that is the traditional home of the Nacotchtank and Piscataway peoples. These peoples and many others were forcibly removed from these lands, and the museum's occupation of these lands is fundamentally tied to colonialism. The author acknowledges the Nacotchtank and Piscataway peoples as the original stewards of this land, and pays respect to past, present, and future generations who continue to live on these lands, and who have been forced from these lands.

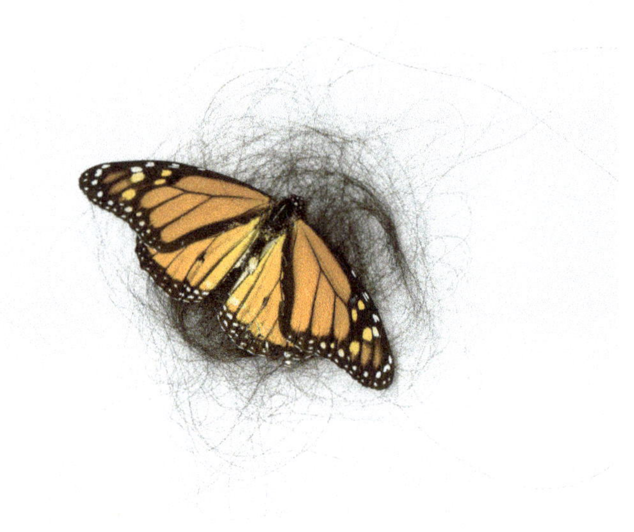

Juan Molina Hernández

el fin y principio u otro tipo de metamorfosis (*the beginning and the end or a different type of metamorphosis*), 2021

Archival inkjet print

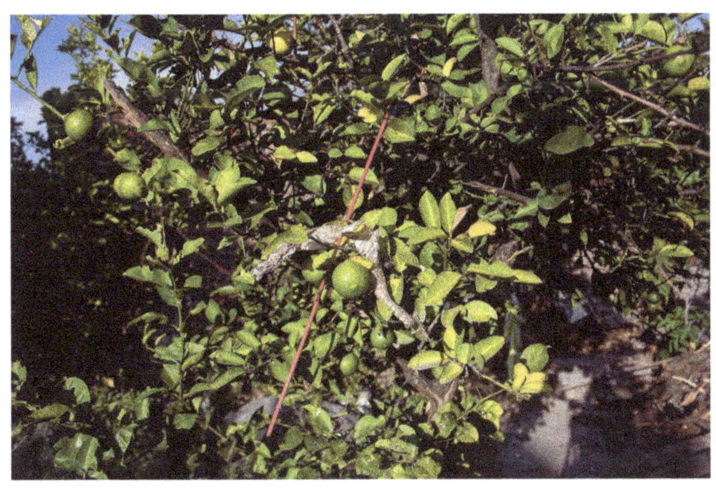

Juan Molina Hernández

autorretrato o piel vieja y lo que sobra de una manda cumplida (self-portrait or old skin and remnants of a prayer answered), 2017

Archival inkjet print

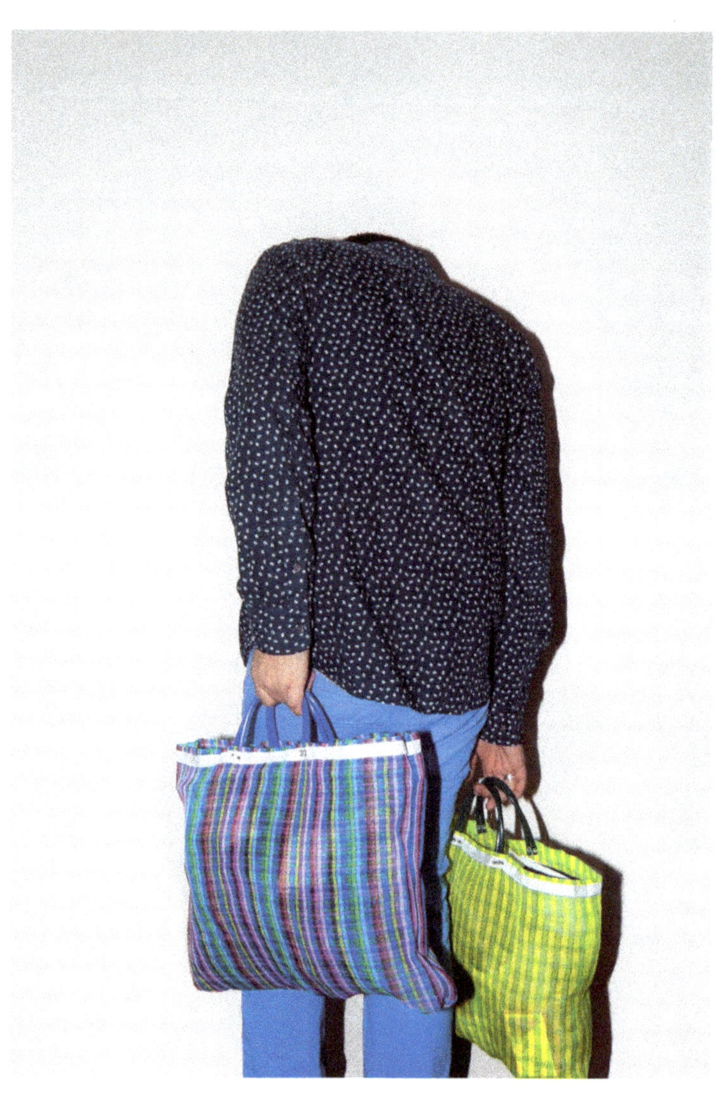

Juan Molina Hernández

cuando te vas (when you leave), 2014

Archival inkjet print

PART 4

TRANSCIENCE

15

MY AUTOBIOGRAPHY OF 'MY AUTOBIOGRAPHY OF CARSON MCCULLERS' BY JENN SHAPLAND

MARLO KOCH

1

"Isn't that what you were looking for?"[1] Jenn Shapland's girlfriend asks her over the phone after Shapland excitedly relays her findings: therapy transcripts of 20th century writer Carson McCullers admitting that she is a lesbian. Until that point, Shapland's archival research taking her from the Ransom Center in Texas to McCullers's home in Ohio had only hinted at the writer's queerness: several important and tumultuous relationships with women recorded as friendships, all during her marriage with her husband.

In response to Chelsea, Shapland's girlfriend, she says "Well, I didn't actually think I'd find it."[2]

2

On a sunny, still Sunday in April, I paced around my apartment and sent a text message:

I want to tell you what happened to me.

Later, I biked to a nearby ice cream shop. Wearing a dress and sneakers, I stood with my bike and watched as a man, my new boyfriend, approached. Eating vanilla cones with sprinkles, we walked, our bikes rolling in tandem between us. At home, we got into bed and I told him my story.

"There are many ways to interpret a life. But what if we choose the most probable scenario, the path of least resistance, instead of trying to talk our way out of what seems evident, instead of trying to explain away the obvious?" Shapland writes.

In my mid-twenties, in the middle of graduate school, I had just completed a very successful run of abusive romantic relationships. It was so successful, in fact, it could have extended for an encore performance. As I transitioned myself from currently-abused to used-to-be-abused, I wondered how to retell these events and how the retelling would change over time. I wondered what proof I would need to produce in order to be believed, in order to align my past with my reality. *Show me the receipts*, I imagined a future partner demanding. I discarded or edited all journal entries from those years, including electronic records. Any clothing from that time has long been resold or trashed. There exists very few photographs of me; I almost never took selfies, for fear that I would be faced with a bodily example of how I was being hurt. For several months, every shower or bath was a transformative scrubbing clean experience of coming back to myself. Eventually, a balancing act began. I walk around with a trick up my sleeve, a trick of holding my disbelief at what happened to me against a desire to communicate my whole self as a form of love.

3

Much like the journey of Shapland's research—meandering, illuminative then dark—*My Autobiography* is told in short, sometimes one-line chapters. Some are focused on McCullers' clothing stored at the Ransom Center: "Clothes make visible what we feel or believe about ourselves even if the identity is invisible to others,"[3] writes Shapland. Others are pulled from Shapland's biography. One details bringing Shapland's first girlfriend—her "roommate"—home and her mother confronting her with her diary entries about the relationship.

In the Chapter "Imaginary Friends," Shapland describes a therapy session in which Mary Mercer, McCullers' therapist, asks whether McCullers and Annemarie Schwarzenbach, a Swiss writer, had slept together. The transcripts have blank spots, ellipses, and pauses. Eventually, through several translations of handwriting and typed text, Mary writes that *yes*, they did sleep together. But this does not satisfy Shapland. "What more proof did I think I needed? What was I trying to prove?"[4]

The arrow that guides Shapland is a belief that if she can believe that McCullers was a lesbian, or loved woman, then her identity is validated. First there is a stumbling, then a discovery, and then a proving in *My Autobiography.* Shapland comes to Maggie Nelson's exploration of her Aunt Jane and her murder. Nelson writes, "I never thought 'my Jane' might approximate the 'real Jane.'"[5] Throughout the reading of *My Autobiography*, I regularly flip to the dedication page that states, "For your Carson." Shapland has come to an acceptance and realization that her Carson is the one that matters. No biographer, family member, or even romantic partner can truly conjure another person no matter how hard they believe they have. Who is a person beyond what they choose to build outwardly? If we cannot take the archive to be true, what do we turn to?

4

A common adage in certain trauma circles is that the body regenerates every seven years, suggesting that one day your physical body will no longer be the same one that was traumatized. Though simplistic and not entirely medically accurate, the inevitability of growth and rebirth as time passes is a comfort. And yet, healing is both nonlinear and unseeable.

McCullers went to therapy in order to write a memoir. Shapland went to therapy at age 25, facing a breakup and her first year in graduate school. To her new therapist, she said, "I seem to have lost the narrative thread of my life."

Walking someone through my past, be it my boyfriend, my therapist, or friends, is a cloudy and ambiguous process. I neglected to talk about it at all for several years, because it was not neatly tied up with a but-now-I-am-better bow. In my retelling, I find myself doubling back, repeating, and reassessing simultaneously. It is like I am measuring fixed points against metrics that have yet to be measured.

5

"There is a desire to know that is already knowing, a curiosity for what you deep down recognize, a lust for what you are or could be,"[6] Shapland writes, describing the beginning, excited stages of her Carson research, which turned out to be the culmination of Carson's life.

McCullers' therapy sessions with Mary Mercer occurred in the last ten years of her life before she died at age 50. Shapland's book, by way of the therapy transcription and other clues (McCullers dedicated her novel, *A Clock Without Hands*, to Mercer), suggests that McCullers and Mercer were in love. Desiring evidence towards truth is human— but that is not how belief or love works.

Near the ending of *My Autobiography*, Shapland describes *Edie* by Jean Stein, an oral history of Edie Sedgwick. "I began to see just how many ways a person's life might be told... It [*Edie*] encompasses the contradicting opinions and stories about its subject's life without trying to recon- cile them."[7] Shapland's suggestion that an amalgamation of a person's life can be contradictory feels like truth. I come back to *show me the receipts*, the idea that someone might require more proof than I am willing to provide, which kept me silent for a long time. But my amalgama- tion, with its blurred edges, has proven to be recognized as the only thing that matters: my truth. To look back on and recreate from archive or memory takes reinvention. But it also takes acceptance of the fallibility of records—that retelling from memory is the only way to move through the future.

16

THE POSSIBILITIES OF MUSEUM-AS-RHIZOME

NINA WHITE

In 2020, museums and researchers alike had to adapt their work and play to new distanced and restricted means. Initially, in the United Kingdom, museums' work felt frozen—suspended temporarily as lockdown restrictions resulted in closures and necessitated a transition from physical, proximate programming to digital delivery of exhibitions and community activities. Through my research at Middlesbrough Institute of Modern Art (MIMA), situated in the North East of England, I have found galleries and museums to be reflective, alternative, and *indeterminate* spaces. Navigating museums research through the pandemic, the concept of the rhizome has been crucial in developing an understanding of the indeterminate, transitory nature of museums, and how knowledge production takes place between artists, museum workers, visitors, constituents and volunteers, "all moving together yet disparately... people, objects, and ideas constantly rotating in and out," seeping out of the museum walls and into public, domestic and digital spaces.[1]

The concept of *museum-as-rhizome* has emerged in my research so far to frame MIMA's community programme. While the concept emerges from site-specific research, it has a potency in its universality, with the rhizome opening up and connecting the gallery to its communities and counterparts across space and time. If museums are rhizomes; ever-growing, connecting, living, breathing maps, Where else can their connections take us? Where, who, and what do they connect to? The rhizome offers an alternative model to examine and appraise museums more broadly, rejecting any form of hierarchical linearity in which knowledge production takes place top-down, from museum to visitor. In the rhizome, knowledge is ever evolving, shifting in mutualistic osmosis between artists, staff, volunteers, constituents, and visitors. Deleuze and Guattari imagine this mutualism of the rhizome in their reinterpretation of the reproduction of orchids. Instead of seeing the wasp that it co-opts into its pollination as a separate entity, they write of a "veritable becoming, a becoming-wasp of the orchid and a becoming-orchid of the wasp."[2] These 'becomings' can also be found in the museum-as-rhizome; from the becoming-artist of the constituent to the becoming-constituent of the curator, in a collective process of knowledge co-production and co-learning.

As Deleuze and Guattari further philosophize on the botanical structure of the rhizome, it becomes an 'image of thought,' offering an alternative way of writing, researching and being (or becoming) which engages and acknowledges multiple ways of knowing. The rhizome 'ceaselessly establishes connections between semiotic chains, organizations of power, and circumstances relative to the arts, sciences, and social struggles.'[3] Deleuze and Guattari expand on the rhizome's characteristics:

…unlike trees or their roots, the rhizome connects any point to any other point, and its traits are not necessarily linked to traits of the same nature; it brings into play very different regimes of signs, and even nonsign states. The rhizome is reducible neither to the One nor the multiple… It has neither beginning nor end, but always a middle (milieu) from which it grows and which it overspills… The rhizome operates by variation, expansion, conquest, capture, and offshoots. Unlike the graphic arts, drawing, or photography, unlike tracings, the rhizome pertains to a map that must be produced, constructed, a map that is always detachable, connectable, reversible, modifiable, and has multiple entryways and exits and its own lines of flight.[4]

As rhizomes, museums, and galleries are reducible neither to their singular buildings or the multiple artworks in their collections. Neither are they reducible to their staff, artists, or visitors. Instead, they are milieus of people, objects, places and actions, that vary, expand and offshoot. They have multiple entryways and exits, ways to encounter and interact, with 'lines of flight' ranging from exhibitions and projects through to conversations and meals. MIMA's rhizomatic indeterminacy can be found in multiple guises. It is referred to variously as both (or either) gallery or museum, with roots in public council ownership. It has been part of Teesside University since 2014 and became MIMA School of Art and Design in 2019. Through its community programme, the gallery space becomes a play-group, a dining hall, a dementia-friendly space, and a language learning classroom. Outside the gallery walls, activities spill over into local residential communities and navigate the locality through a mobile plant and activity 'barrow.'

The multiplicity of museums means they cannot be comprehended using methods designed for study of the individual. By turning from qualitative research to post-qualitative inquiry, museums research can embrace "the always already more than, too big of inquiry…too strange to count as science…the provocation, the knot, the world kicking back, the too much that demands experimentation."[5] From the ground-breaking writings of Elizabeth Adams St Pierre, other researchers have taken up the challenge of post qualitative inquiry to offer up new approaches including 'kitchen research practices,' 'philosophical fieldnotes,' and 'inquiry on the sly.'[6] Kuntz and Guyotte respond to this messy excess with their practice of 'inquiry-play' which 'necessarily occurs in indeterminate spaces, manifesting through the excessive enactments of action.'[7] Inquiry-play, then, is also a match for the knots and provocations of museums work manifesting in indeterminate spaces. Play is intrinsic to MIMA's civic mission *Art in Action*, instigated through creative activity between "artists and communities on projects that raise debate, open discussion and generate new possibilities…[and] address urgent issues such as climate change, migration, inequality, ageing, social isolation, wellbeing, and relations between people and the world's natural resources."[8]

The complex museum ecology referenced in MIMA's mission statement reflects what Jennifer Greene describes as the 'flat topology' of post qualitative research. For Greene, the world is "not just a 'social' world… rather, human interactions, thoughts, language/discourse, matter (materiality), and nature are all occupants of this world— referred to as an assemblage or mangle in post qualitative writing—and all have equal status in this world's flat topology."[9] This same concept of a flat topology can be applied to museums. In the museum-as-rhizome, human interactions and their thoughts, language and discourse—whether gallery staff, constituents, artists, or visitors co-exist with the artworks, building, and nature. Like all museums, MIMA's existence relies as much on its visitors from near and far as it does its artists, its collections, its teachers, its students, and its staff. The delicate ecology of this assemblage requires the equal status of each component, living and nonliving, human, and non-human.

Unlike more conventional methodologies, post qualitative inquiry embraces the non-living and non-human. [10] In the case of museums, the non-living and non-human can encompass the physical buildings, collections, ecosystems, and even digital outputs and engagements, which have grown exponentially during the global pandemic. MIMA, for example, responded to restrictions with a new digital programme including an online community zine and artist interview series, virtual creative activity sessions for families, artist studio visits, and an online exhibition. Through such digital activities, museums are continuously encountering, merging, and becoming with another much larger rhizome: cyberspace. Vieira and Ferasso describe cyberspace—or 'the web'—as "not only the material infrastructure of digital communication, but also the sea of information that it encompasses as well as the human beings who sail in and feed this universe."[11] Its interconnection "constitutes humankind in a continuum without borders, immersing beings and things in the same path of interactive communication."[12] The web's endless links, connections and pathways, and the collective intelligence that it sets into motion, lead Vieira and Ferasso to the conclusion that "cyberspace is shaped like Deleuze–Guattari's rhizome... if we replaced the word 'rhizome' with 'cyberspace', the result would be practically the same."[13]

Cyberspace has come to play an even larger role in daily lives everywhere as pandemic restrictions continue to disrupt daily activities that previously relied on face-to-face interactions, producing a new terminology for and experience of 'the new normal.' In-person conversations and meetings have been replaced by video conferencing—even pub quizzes take place virtually—and, in my experience as a researcher, disruption of library services and campus access has rendered my research almost entirely reliant on the internet. Reading Vieira and Ferasso's writing ten years after publication, it is clear that the rhizomatic nature of cyberspace has been exacerbated and accelerated by the conditions of the pandemic. In cyberspace, "practical operation projects can be performed in digital environments, personal relationships can become stronger due to virtual ties and virtual communities can set into motion a collective intelligence capable of reaching new levels of knowledge."[14] This virtualisation also means that organisations "are less and less dependent on location, established working hours and long-term planning."[15]

This surge in online use and activity has been matched in the world of academia by a proliferation of virtual conferences, online talks and webinars. It is unsurprising then, that some of the most compelling writings on museums, the arts, and activism would come from cyberspace. Spaces such as the online "unconference" series, *Death to Museums,* and creative critical platform, *The White Pube,* demonstrate the internet's crucial role, not only as tool and forum but as a plane of existence for critical thought.[16] The democratisation of knowledge made possible by the world wide web and its many rabbit holes does not problematise research quality but enhances and improves it. Google Docs, blog posts, and podcasts only serve to make knowledge, discussion, and dialogue more open, more accessible, and more interconnected than ever before. Existing within a global rhizomatic structure, these experimental and creative digital sources of discussion map onto the aims of post qualitative inquiry and can be considered equally alongside so-called academic literature. In the same way that the flat topology of the museum confronts hierarchies of knowledge production in the museum space, so too does the flat topology of cyberspace destabilise hierarchies of knowledge production in academia.

Just as the various turns in qualitative research have rested on global change and mass upheaval, the shift in my own research from qualitative methodology to post qualitative *anti*-methodology, was triggered by the global upheaval caused by the COVID-19 pandemic of 2020.[17] I was drawn to the flexibility and creativity of post qualitative inquiry, which "doesn't have pre-existing methods of data analysis like coding data or thematic analysis… [and] refuses representationalist logic."[18] In the new world of restrictions and distancing, a methodology embracing and seeking strangeness and 'the world kicking back' seemed the only route to navigate my research. According to Deleuze and Guattari, the multiplicity of the rhizome cannot grow without changing in nature.[19] My research couldn't grow without changing into something "visceral, tearful and bruising, filled with laughter and hugs, fully engaged in intra-action."[20] The emotive viscerality of post qualitative inquiry is at odds with the rigidity and order that conventional qualitative methodology attempts to bring to a world where neither exists. The world does not recognise methodology. The world recognises disorder, spontaneity, and even chaos as 2020 has attested to. The so-called objective researcher, remaining detached from subjects and interviewees, had no place in the new normal.

While the figuration of the rhizome enables crucial moments of excess and play to be captured, both pre-pandemic in-person and new digital and distanced work, it is far from the perfect analogy for museums. As Deleuze and Guattari warn, "even when one thinks one has reached a multiplicity, it may be a false one—of what we call the radicle type—because its ostensibly nonhierar-chical presentation or statement in fact only admits of a totally hierarchical solution."[21] Use of the rhizome concept in museum research is not to say that the museum holds 'true' Deleuzoguattarian multiplicity. Rather, it tests out the use of philosophy-as-method in museum work, challenging the problematic hierarchies that still persist in twenty-first century museums and galleries. It celebrates the possibili-ties of digital-real rhizomatic working as a "process [that] makes room for individual manifestations, which soon become collective… [where] art is created, the world is built, languages mingle and democracy prevails"[22] and seeks to complicate the binary of museum and visitor.

17

WHAT IF MUSEUMS WORKED LIKE LIBRARIES?

HANNAH BAKER

In mid-2020, I watched a recording of an Allied Media Conference in which Alexis Pauline Gumbs invited us in the YouTube audience to write from the edge of our imaginations, to write from the edge of the best thing we could think.[1] This is my experiment in doing so. I ask the question What if museums worked like libraries? to open my mental door to what else museums could be, knowing that some museums do indeed work like libraries right now. I invite the reader to think joyfully with me about the future of art and people together.

10 years after museums in New York City deaccessioned their collections, museum spaces worked like libraries. They lent art works to people's homes, classrooms, gardens, and sidewalks. They also hosted community events that were open, free, and by and for the people. These folks knew what it was to care for something sacred, to have a gift, and a responsibility.[2]

Come, museums urged, check out a moment in time, take it home, explore it, and read it closely. Give it an adventure to tell the next guest. Hold it. Smell it. Return it and try another one. Hang a portrait on your wall. Fill your home with color and texture and when you need a refresh, come peruse our holds and find something new, or take a break in our halls. Shake off your coat and nestle in the holds of the collections. Touch something kindly. Look upon something else and sit. These new places are free spaces, which are open 24 hours a day to anyone who would like to come in and be.

"Come," said the art. We are lonely and sore and tired of one another, and our lonely and sore neighbors. We long for a toddler's sticky hands, smudged with jam. We are not afraid of being damaged or being used. Things are fixable, flexible, and we want to gather stories in our cracks. Some of us will be damaged greatly, but that is okay. We want to move and breathe and talk to new faces and new places. We are vibrant and ready for something else; something other than these great halls and white boxes.

The Pink Bike

I am a bike. A pink bike, with foxtails dangling from my handles. There are about 200 others like me, self-propelling and energy conserving machines. Ride me downhill and I save up your momentum and I can push us up the next hill. Apparently I was costly to produce—too costly for the mass production that would signify the success of a commodity. I am a bike that makes no messes. I have spent a long time in the Brooklyn Museum in a glass box propped up with some material. I'm not even using my kickstand, which is the thing designed to help me stay up when I am no longer in motion. My leather seat is empty, and has been empty for so long.

When did I last feel anything? Any wind, rain, or breeze? When did I last hear a bird, a whoosh, or a pant? When last did I move, really move with someone else? I am lonely and I am alone, isolated, and untouched. Certainly, I am not rusted nor dusty. My chain is unbroken and my gears shift just fine. But does it matter? Does it really matter that I am preserved and yet unused? I am unridden and sore. I may not work anymore. I could be broken and no one would know.

The Converting Chair

I am a converting chair. I live in the same room as the pink bike. At least here there is light, and some people come and look sometimes. I am a fabulous chair, and also a ladder. People can sit on me. People can climb me to reach something; usually a book. I used to live in a library and there were books all around and sometimes, when things were quiet, I could hear them whisper to one another, whisper their stories and the story behind their stories, their creation stories.

I am made of wood and leather. I was a tree and a cow before I was what I am now. Before that, I was sunlight and water. Now I am not allowed to touch those things, sunlight and water, trees or cows, or grass. Once, some people made a movie about me. It is a short movie, just a few minutes. The movie shows me converting; becoming something new and then returning to my chair form. Sometimes I wonder if I am a ladder who is also a chair, or a chair that is also a ladder, or if maybe I am a few different things. Right now, I am tired of being here next to other chairs (I guess I am a chair). All of us are stacked on shelves, right up to the ceiling.

How Many Collective Years Had These Artworks Spent In Dark Confines, On Shelves and In Drawers and Hung Too Close Together? How Long Had They Sat In Dust and Stagnation?

These artworks had been lonely for too long. They were untouched and unbreathed upon. Centuries after being made, being lovingly held and molded and coaxed and invited into this world, they sat guarded and unheld, observed and separated from those they loved, and those that loved them. Centuries after willing themselves into being, impacting places and spaces, they were relegated to the basement, to storage, and to darkness.

> A spoon unused,
> a chair that sits empty on a shelf, next to
>   other empty chairs,
> a bike unridden, and a clock unwound.
> This is not a life.
> Paintings in purgatory,
> looking at one another
> in the dark.
> What do these artworks say in the dark?
> Who listens?

How Many Items In The NYC Museum Collections Need To Be Returned To Someone Else, Somewhere Else?

Some artworks and artifacts, the community decided, were not for checking out. Bodies, gods, living folk have been trapped for centuries, living underground and separated from their worlds. Pieces of households, of family history, are separated by walls, security, rituals, and oceans away from what they were made for. Their life cycles are interrupted by a need to know something completely, a belief that this knowing is ethical, or even possible.

Some of these artworks were deaccessioned completely. The items, some cracked and stained, others worn, were released into the hands of people to whom they belonged and others into the hands of citizens who were willing to provide the correct care. The museums lost track of some things. This is okay. We can trust our neighbors to do what is right with things we may not understand. Tracking and tracing are not always the responsible moves. In this way, the museum became unlike the library. The museum taught us the lesson that many people already knew: we do not need to gaze upon everything and we do not need to hold everything ourselves to know its value and importance. Meaning is not made in stasis and stagnation in a bid for complete and utter knowing. Sometimes not knowing is honorable.

For many works, returning proved difficult. Nation states are not solid beings, they are viscous borders, absorbing and repelling people and culture. People move, and we still do not know everything of pasts that were erased. Some of these artworks are still tended to as they wait in anticipation of a great return. There is a wake, a watchfulness, and a mourning that is necessary.[3] Some of these artworks cannot be returned. There will be no home going. This caretaking role that museums now pay people to do is a job, the only job really; to steward these works, these people, these gods, and these evidences of life.

What Have Museums Been Used for Now?

Museums are being used for impromptu music halls, dance studios, workshops, organizing spaces, and sometimes still exhibitions, which are community led. They are used for temporary housing, permanent housing, teach-ins, funerals, weddings, family bonding, respite, holiday celebrations, graduations, sitting and looking, green houses and rooftop gardens, for pop-up restaurants, and communal meals.

What Have Museum Staff Done?

Art guards have become the backbone of the museum-as-library. As those who spent the most time in the gallery, watching the community and watching the art, they know things about the visitors of the artworks. Education staff now collaborates with the community. Who knows what? Who can teach something to a group? What skills are needed? What tools are needed? The conservator's mission has changed. It's no longer to keep a work as it was, but to let it be what it is and repair if necessary, wipe down, clean up, give it a kiss, and let it rest. Curators do this work too by talking with the community and caring for objects. In fact, most of the roles have blurred, meeting new needs, and allowing for flexibility and responsiveness. Board members are no longer part of the museum's ecosystem. Community members guide and ask questions of the museum, lay forth plans, and help to allocate funds.

Where Are These Museums Going Now?

The museums continue to shift and embrace the ever-changing needs of an ever-changing community. The new museum embraces not knowing, asking questions, and changing. Flexibility and community care guide us and people of the new museums into the future.

Author's Note

This work is in progress, a set of ideas and fabulations, which will change as I read and listen to more and share this story with others. Nearly every time I talk through this idea, someone mentions a museum that is already working in this way giving me something more to explore and expand my ways of thinking about the role of the museum and what art stewardship looks like. It is my hope that this story invites a new way for us all to relate to the objects we interact with daily, to appreciate and care for those things that live with us and that may have lived with others before. Caring and repairing invites us to think with objects and ultimately with the people and planet that have made them, increasing our sense of connection to one another and the places where we live.

I was inspired by Death to Museum's most recent virtual panel, *Indigenous Knowledge & Cultural Work*, a wonderful conversation between Heidi K. Brandow, Courtney Little Axe, and Jordan Poorman Cocker, which challenged me to expand my understanding of repatriation.[4] The first question of the museum-as-library moved me towards a broader understanding of what is not acceptably held in the museum collection, and what is not acceptable to be lent out like a library book. Additionally, ideas about museum function, form, and fantastic imagination have come from Kimberly Drew's *This is What I Know About Art* and Eve Kosofsky Sedgwick's "Paranoid Reading and Reparative Reading, Or You're So Paranoid You Probably Think This Introduction is About You."[5] Taken together, a call for something different is clear. This is my contribution to the conversation which looks toward a different museum.

18

ALWAYS MOVING FORWARD
MEMORIES OF SOUTH ASIA FACEBOOK GROUP

SANA SABOOWALA

Diasporic South Asians know about transitory existence. We did not lose lives, or dignity, or security in our migrations. We only lost dolls, wedding albums, and a sense of belonging. We are the lucky ones. So-called "third culture kids" (second and third generation immigrants) identify with movement too as they navigate code-switching, the act of switching between home culture and more socially acceptable—usually Western—language. Diasporic South Asian knowledge of migration does not come from textbooks, museums, or sensationalized narratives of nationalist glory. It comes from everyday memories; the memories we hear of in-season fruits, favorite toys, and childhood playmates, and the memories we have of homemade food, family holidays, and mispronounced names. It comes from witnessing the nostalgia for a past that exists beyond man-made borders. These everyday memories give us roots.

When the global pandemic limited our movement, the desire to reflect on past migrations came to light. Families started living in close quarters, while elderly people became more socially isolated. The needs of the community, especially a need to connect with elderly people, became apparent. Born from a desire to engage intergenerationally with the powerful memories of everyday life, the *Memories of South Asia*[1] project formed around migration, movement, and the 1947 border creation event that divided the subcontinent into the states of India and Pakistan, known as Partition. Each month, members vote on a theme, discuss memories surrounding that theme with family and friends, and post their discussions. People have posted videos talking to their grandchildren about favorite childhood foods, pictures of their childhood homes, and comments about fond memories. This space serves as an archive of communal memory. Members curate their own content and share their own stories in monthly exhibits. They decide what we discuss, and there is no institutional hierarchy to minimize the power of lived experience. In a society inundated with propaganda about the 'other,' this space reminds us that people's lives tell a different story. This movement away from institutional narratives is one of the multidimensional ways the Memories of South Asia Facebook group engages with transit. The specters of migration stemming from the trauma of the 1947 Partition continue to impact South Asians today and show up in stories of everyday life.[2] Furthermore, the group moves beyond Facebook into the sphere of day-to-day interactions. Finally, the participatory space works to transcend binaries and boundaries.

The discussion of the everyday reflects our displacement and serves as a tool towards accepting that dislocation. Third culture kids need everyday stories, because they help us to turn to our roots when Western society rejects us.

Everyday memories show us that however far we move, roots still stay strong. When I ask elders in my community about mundane aspects of their past, like what their childhood home looked like, they often respond with "why bother asking about that?" They do not understand the power of their everyday stories. They do not know that people want to listen; that their past still impacts our future. Children and grandchildren often do not think to ask about the past. They don't always realize that talking to their grandparents provides more cultural knowledge than visiting a museum. Museums undervalue the knowledge held by community members as well. Museums provide 'authorized' versions of history that become public memory; they serve as a form of official memory like textbooks and state archives[3]. The narratives in these places are 'worked' to support existing power structures, not the lived experiences of the average person[4]. The narratives in these institutions are selected. The Memories of South Asia Facebook group, in contrast, showcases all storytelling. The group aims to complicate institutional narratives by including more voices and encouraging oral transmission via intergenerational conversations. Oral historians have demonstrated the value of listening to peoples' stories[5]. Colonial institutions teach us that our everyday lives are not worth preserving, unlike the thoughts of 'great white men.' The Memories of South Asia Facebook group emphasizes individual stories by demonstrating what conversations about the past can look like. For instance, I encouraged a friend to ask his grandmother about her memories of the first Independence Day in India using the loose template provided in the group and to post about it after. My friend was hesitant, but he learned things about his grandmother that no one in the family had known, because no one had thought to ask. It brought him closer to his roots. The Facebook group, and the conversations sparked through it, show that people don't need an institution to tell them their stories are important. This group has its own limitations, including requiring internet access and a Facebook account, which could make it more difficult to access for some people than local museums. It also does not have the protection of anonymity or privacy the way participatory exhibits at museums may have. Although online community spaces like the Memories of South Asia Facebook group have some drawbacks, they offer dynamic possibilities, even outside of the online realm.

Conversations and cultural exchanges move beyond the virtual boundaries of Facebook. The exposure to everyday narratives reminds people to ask about the past in their day-to-day interactions; the global pandemic has created space for these reflections as families lock down together. Since the creation of this group, I have seen the change in my own family. For instance, my aunt and mother told me about their childhood home because the topic popped up on my aunt's Facebook feed. These conversations are oral transmissions of knowledge. The oral tradition begins with holding space for family tradition passed on through these conversations. The colonial focus on enlightenment *objectivity* pushes society to discount oral histories as too *subjective*. As scholar Janet Linde points out, people 'work' stories to reflect their interests, in written text and oral conversations.[6] Thus, objectivity stands in for the white Protestant male perspective. Everyday conversation, more than media, shapes our identities and our culture. Some, like my aunt, prefer to restrict the intergenerational conversations that come up through the Memories of South Asia Facebook group to private conversations within the family. People like her choose not to share, but still privately engage with the posts. Even 'lurkers,'people who look at posts but never comment or react, benefit from the creation of this forum as it inspires conversation elsewhere in life. This platform serves as a way for diasporic South Asians to reflect on our own identities beyond the Facebook group. Since traditional museums base themselves around objects and space, the provocative conversations evoked through exhibits are constrained by artificial boundaries imposed by the structures of limited, colonial institutions. The Memories of South Asia Facebook group creates a setting that facilitates conversations that move beyond those constraints. The conversations created by the group are as diasporic as the people engaging with it. They move and change in multiple settings, from the public Facebook group, to the intimate privacy of people's homes.

Discussing the everyday in a participatory virtual space interrupts the static narratives of state institutions. For instance, in a post about Durga Puja (Figure 1), two women of different nationalities, generations, and religions reflect on celebrating the Bengali holiday. They discuss a shared experience even though it was not contemporaneous or even in the same location; collective remembering occurred across binary lines (Indian/Pakistani, Millennial/Generation X, and Hindu/Muslim). The Memories of South Asia Facebook group serves as a reflective space where people can have these experiences of collective remembering in a casual, low-pressure context, which causes the lines of manmade institutionalized binaries to shift and blur.

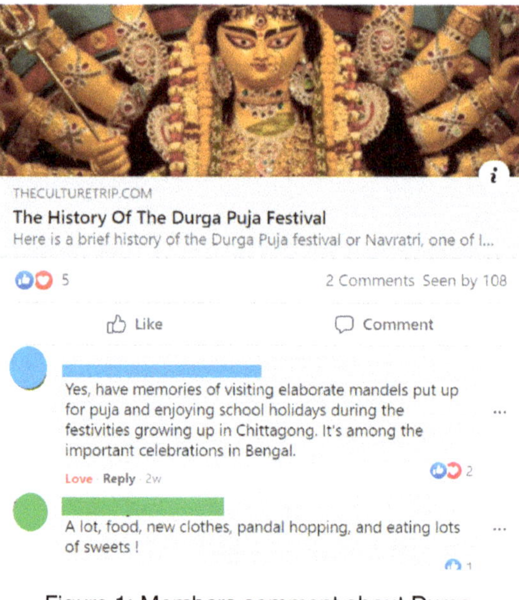

Figure 1: Members comment about Durga Puja in the Memories of South Asia Facebook Group (screenshot with paint to protect privacy). Captured on December 22, 2020.

Furthermore, people feel comfortable inserting knowledge to fill in gaps that exist in public memory. As established, public memory reflects people in power rather than the collective. The casual format of the group allows people to share their own stories and point to missing perspectives without pressure. For example, when the theme for the month was "food memories," one user posted about Dalit food and noted that Dalit foodways have systemically been erased from conversations about South Asian food. The participatory format encourages users to fill in gaps. Our institutions rely on "authorized" memories and knowledge to develop narratives to present to the public.[7] This process takes a long time to adapt to new information or viewpoints. The dynamic of the Facebook group allows a plurality of voices to speak on an issue, and does not gatekeep which voices may take up space. Drawing from Sandra Harding's idea of standpoint epistemologies, the Facebook group aims to create space for people to share a variety of viewpoints publicly to move away from monolithic narratives about the past. The Facebook group changes with new knowledge in a transparent way. For instance, I made a post about a childhood game called koladaam. I had thought it was played like another Gujrati game known as dadu. Members commented, correcting my mistake and posting photos of the koladaam board (Figure 2). This iterative, public, in-real-time correction reflects how quickly knowledge can, and should be, expanded.

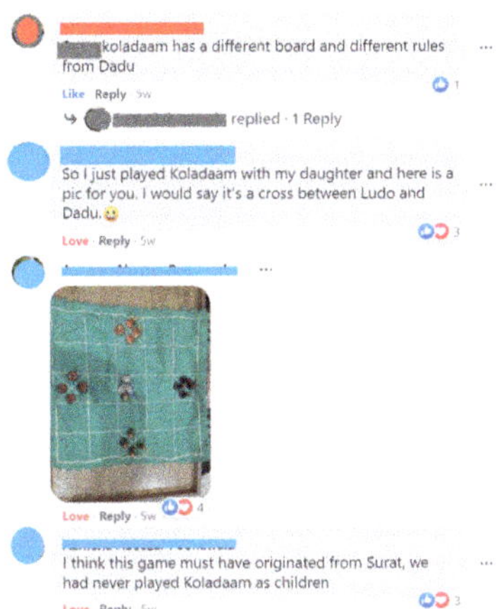

Figure 2: Members comment about koladaam in the Memories of South Asia Facebook Group (screenshot with paint to protect privacy). Captured on December 22, 2020.

Alternative spaces like the Memories of South Asia Facebook group will continue to provide places for people to engage in cultural exchange, reflection, and memory-making. As the Facebook group grows, more people with different perspectives will post in the group, improving the knowledge shared by the space, strengthening the conversations people have, and diversifying the content to meet the needs of members. As a transitory space, the group always changes, because its membership and their stories continually shift. This reflective space helps diasporic South Asians engage with their cultural identity. It also serves as an alternative space for cultural memory-making that is beyond museums or static digital archives. To preserve cultural memory, we do not need museums. We need people to share their knowledge. People can discuss their objects and stories without ceding ownership. The Memories of South Asia space will change and grow with the people it serves. That's the best part about transitory spaces; they look back while always moving forward.

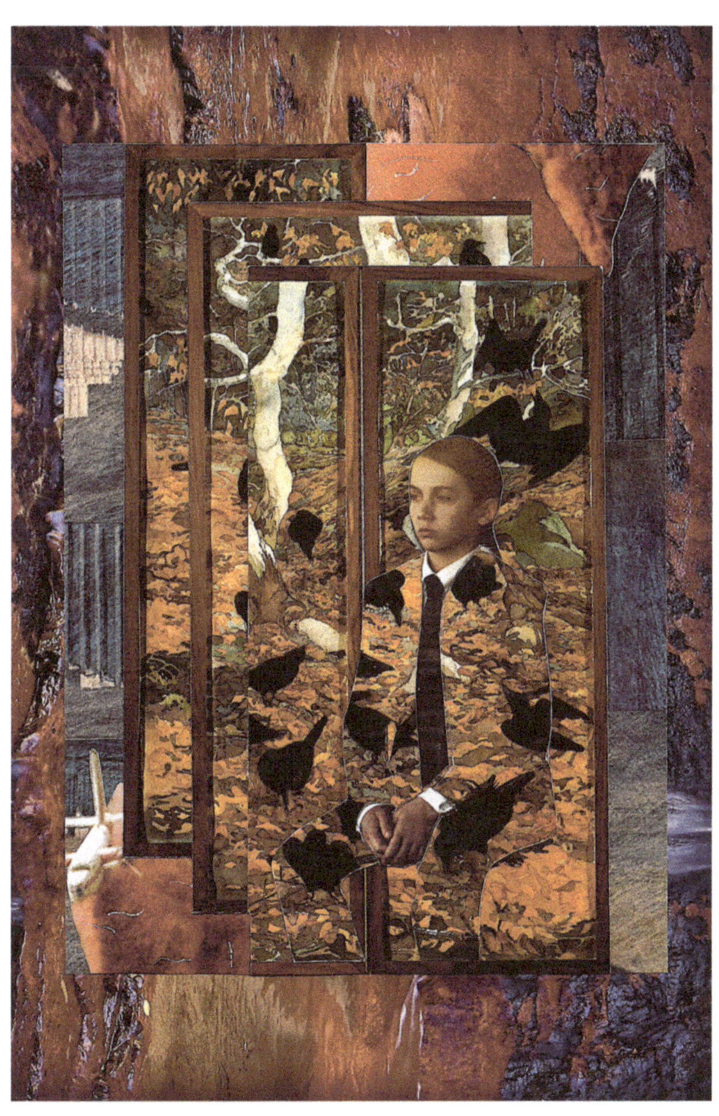

Graham Neff

Slow Shift, 2021

Analog collage

"I CREATED this piece with the idea of change and transition and the idea that it is fast and slow; it is constant and inevitable. The child is moving forward with age while the environment around them decays. Ravens are typically associated with some sort of doom, but they also relate to prophecy. I like this duality and tried to reflect that in the collage design and color palette. We are always transitioning. It's good to remind ourselves that the rest of the world is too."

CONTRIBUTOR BIOS

Azubuike Akunne is an enigmatic creative and entrepreneur currently living in Lagos, Nigeria. When in Chicago, Azubuike is heavily involved in the food justice space with his company NeuBite and looks to technology to help solve problems facing society. Azubuike received his B.S. in Human Nutrition from The Ohio State University and a Masters in Business Administration from Chicago's Roosevelt University.

Kaelyn Andrade is a Chicago-based artist. She is currently attending the University of Illinois at Chicago (UIC), double majoring in Art and Art History with a minor in Museum and Exhibition Studies. Andrade works primarily in 2D materials such as paint and charcoal. Her work surrounds her experience and knowledge of Mexican history and identity. Andrade is invested in understanding the development of Mexican identity throughout history and often fuses historical imagery with contemporary ones to create connections and understanding of the past. In addition to her studies at UIC, Andrade has worked as a

Museum Educator for the past five years at the National Museum of Mexican Art. There she creates programming, leads workshops and tours, and creates virtual content surrounding Mexican culture. Insta: @kaelyn_artwork @kaelyn_andrade

Hannah Baker is a graduate student in New York, where she studies alternative forms of art stewardship. She loves reading speculative fiction, playing games with her partner, and taking walks in her neighborhood.

Ionit Behar is Assistant Curator at DePaul Art Museum (DPAM), Chicago. She also teaches art history at the School of the Art Institute of Chicago and serves as the Director of Curatorial Affairs for the non-profit Fieldwork Collaborative Projects. Prior to joining DPAM, she was the Curator of Collections and Exhibitions at Spertus Institute for Jewish Learning and Leadership, a Research Assistant for the exhibition Hélio Oiticica: To Organize Delirium at the Art Institute of Chicago, and a Graduate Curatorial Assistant at Gallery 400, University of Illinois at Chicago. Her writing has appeared in exhibition catalogues and art journals such FIELD: A Journal of Socially-Engaged Art Criticism, The Chicago Reader, THE SEEN, and The Exhibitionist. Born in Israel and raised in Uruguay, Behar is a PhD candidate in Art History at the University of Illinois at Chicago and her dissertation is titled Intimate Space and the Public Sphere: Margarita Paksa in Argentina's Military Dictatorship.

Rafaela Brosnan recently earned her Master's degree from the University of Chicago with a specialization in Near Eastern Art and Archaeology and Curatorial Studies. Her thesis work focused on ivories from Khorsabad and

Nimrud, and she is interested in how the displacement of objects impacts contemporary interpretations.

Sidney del Ray Murphy is a 2nd year graduate in the Museum and Exhibition Studies program. She has been dedicated to museum and cultural work for over 6 years, working in many cultural and museum spaces during that time. Sidney has two cats, Hall and Oates, who are "chonky" boys.

Melissa Forstrom, PhD is an assistant professor at Purchase College- State University of New York, where she teaches about the intersections of museology, visual culture, and arts management. She coedited and contributed to Museum Innovation: Building More Equitable, Relevant and Impactful Museums (Routledge, forthcoming 2021) and authored "Museum Maps and the Edge" (Media Fields, 2019). Melissa has been an invited lecturer at the University of Leicester, University of Oslo, and Humboldt University, amongst many others. Having presented her research at conferences in the USA, UK, Germany, Singapore, and Russia, she has also been invited to speak at numerous art institutions.

Abby Foss has a background in Art History and Arts Management, and is a recent graduate of Museum and Exhibition Studies at the University of Illinois at Chicago. She has been in transit all her life, having moved multiple times across the country, and she hopes to settle here in Chicago for a while before the next big move.

Daniel P. Graham is a historian, educator, museum professional, and writer, currently working as the Coordinator of Education and Outreach at the College Park Aviation Museum, and as an Adjunct Professor at Hood College, teaching courses in Public History. Dr. Graham's research interests include issues of equity and pedagogy in public history, as well as the development of science, technology, and medicine in the nineteenth century, and the intersections of technology, business, culture, and individual agency in history.

Ramsey Hoey is a recent graduate of the Museum and Exhibition Studies program at the University of Illinois at Chicago. She graduated from the University of North Dakota with a B.F.A in Studio Art with minors in Art History and Graphic Design. In her graduate studies, she is working toward creating a digital platform for emerging artists.

Larsen Husby is an interdisciplinary artist, working across media to examine themes of place, mapping, and belonging. In conjunction with his personal practice, he co-founded the nonprofit Minneapolis Art Lending Library in 2013. He received his MFA in Studio Arts from the University of Illinois at Chicago in 2020 and his BA in Studio Art from Macalester College in 2012. He currently lives and works in Chicago.

Jessica Johnson is a PhD student at UC Berkeley. She holds a BA and MA in Art History and a certification in Museum Studies. She has worked within the museological field for the past ten years. Her future pursuits include interconnections between Egyptology, digital humanities, and museum outreach and administration.

Marlo Koch is a Chicago-based writer currently serving as the Managing Editor of Chicago Artists Writers (CAW) as well as an editor at Funny Looking Dog Quarterly. Koch holds an MFA in Studio Art from the University of Illinois at Chicago. Her poems have been published by Peach Mag, Sobotka Literary Magazine, Hole Black Hole Catalog, Funny Looking Dog Quarterly, among others, and nominated for a Pushcart Prize.

Kacie Martinez-Valle was born and raised in the city of Chicago. Her interests in museum work are largely impacted by her community and city life. Her focus in the museum and art history field is driven by the goal to recontextualize colonial narratives of the Indigenous Americas that have historically favored Western perspectives.

Margaret Middleton is an independent exhibit designer whose work resides at the intersection of design and social justice. Currently based in Belfast, Northern Ireland, Middleton has a degree in industrial design from the Rhode Island School of Design and over 15 years of experience working in the museum field. Middleton developed the Family Inclusive Language Chart in 2014 and consults with museums on implementing family inclusive practice. Their writing has been published in the Journal of Museum Education, Museums & Social Issues, Exhibition (NAME), Dimensions (ASTC), and Museum magazine (AAM).

Juan Molina Hernández, born in Guanajuato, México, is a Chicago-based visual artist. Molina Hernández's art practice primarily uses photography to create narratives that address the complexities of the hybrid immigrant identity. By appropriating symbols from the environment, culture, and personal memory they construct stories in relation to place, family, and a culture that never speaks one language.

Ximena Mora Y Oliván is a Mexican-born naturalized American. They believe in encouraging others to seek participatory and interdisciplinary approaches in cultural work to foster uncommon conversations. Their stewardship practice aims to reintegrate implicit narratives of migration, displacement, queerness, and class dynamics through a blend of personal experience, institutional critique, and archival exploration. They have worked to increase access to ethnographic collections tied to the 1893 World's Fair (Logan Museum of Anthropology, Art Institute of Chicago) as well as intergenerational methodology to local community-based collections (National Museum of Mexican Art). Ximena is featured in an episode of the podcast Wattz's Up! Listen here: https://podcasts.apple.com/us/podcast/wattz-up-open-access-to-the-nmma/id1223817530?i=1000442859999

Henry Morales was born in 1993 in Los Angeles, California. He received his Associates of Arts from the College of Southern Nevada in 2018 and his Bachelor of Fine Arts with an emphasis in Painting at Temple University at The Tyler School of Art and Architecture. His experience as a first-generation Guatemalan American informs much of his practice, which, in turn, allows him to explore themes of labor, immigration, identity, and place.

Alex Orfirer Maher (she/hers) hails originally from Oakland, California and earned her BA in Sociology and Gender & Sexuality Studies from Seattle University. There she became fascinated with how social messaging can shape conceptions of self. She has a particular interest in working creatively and expansively to shape empowered and nuanced Jewish identities. She is currently pursuing her MA in Museum and Exhibition Studies at University of Illinois at Chicago.

Rachel Murphy-Weast is a museum educator in Richmond, Virginia (Powhatan land), whose work at the Virginia Museum of History & Culture centers around digital education and outreach. In 2019, she received state funding to research and develop programs about the women's suffrage centennial. Rachel also peer reviews for The Museum Scholar and serves on the Children's Museum of Richmond's Associate Board. In her free time, Rachel can be found baking or curating her latest to-read list.

Graham Neff is a maker and artist from Coeur d'Alene, Idaho. He specializes in handmade books and analog collage. Currently he resides in his hometown producing artwork and clothing at his small press, The Folded Fox Press. Graham's work aims to explore associations between color and form as well as creating something that is one of a kind. He can be found under the moniker, merlinsfingers, on Instagram.

Therese Quinn (she/they), Director of Museum and Exhibition Studies and Affiliated Faculty with Gender & Women's Studies and Curriculum Studies, has worked as an exhibit researcher, developer, and evaluator for the Field Museum of Natural History, the Chicago Children's Museum, the California Academy of the Sciences, and other cultural institutions. She is the co-editor, with Tuula Juvonen, University of Turku, Finland, of Queer History Month, Journal of Queer Studies in Finland (The Society for Queer Studies in Finland, 2020), and the author of School: Questions About Museums, Culture and Justice to Explore in Your Classroom (2020, Teachers College Press).

Sana Saboowala is a PhD candidate in integrative biology at the University of Illinois Urbana-Champaign. She studies the ways in which memory and trauma are embodied, with a focus on the Partition of South Asia in 1947. More broadly, she aims to take a multidisciplinary approach to research, drawing on the humanities to more deeply answer questions that are traditionally seen as scientific. Her interests include postcolonial STS, critical theory, museum studies, and borderland studies.

Laura Sato grew up in Georgia and graduated from Agnes Scott College with a B.A. in Art History and Women's, Gender, and Sexuality Studies. Laura is finishing up her MA in Museum and Exhibition Studies at UIC. Laura is in transition, enduring an unprecedented global pandemic, and is looking forward to a more inclusive and accessible future. Her research focuses on making museums and art institutions more inclusive, accessible, and engaging for all. You can typically find Laura either reading, drinking iced coffees and lattes, traveling, visiting museums, enjoying theatre, or scrolling through social media.

Quinton Sledge is a graduate of the Museum and Exhibition Studies Program living in the Bucktown neighborhood of Chicago. He made the transition from a small-town Southern Illinois upbringing, to mid-size Central Illinois college town, and landed in the state's bustling Northern metropolis. His time in the MUSE program focused on outreach, education, and interpretation in museums and cultural sites. His final project for his master's degree is centered on a large archive of his great-grandmother's photographs and her mysterious murder 70 years ago. He is also a passionate birdwatcher.

Zoe Silverman is a PhD student at UC Berkeley. She holds a BA and AM in History, an MA M.A. in Learning and Visitor Studies and a certification in Social Emotional Arts. She has worked in the museum field, specifically education, for the past ten years.

Austin Stiegemeier is from Rathdrum, Idaho and was educated in the Pacific Northwest. He has a Bachelor of Fine Arts in Painting and Printmaking from Western Washington University and earned his Master of Fine Arts from Washington State University. Austin taught studio art courses at a number of colleges in Eastern Washington and the Inland Northwest before relocating to Pennsylvania where he works as Assistant Professor of Painting at Gettysburg College. His achievements have been recognized with both state and national awards and he has exhibited his artwork nationally. A number of his artworks are held in private collections in the United States and Europe.

Manon Thompson has lived in the suburbs of Chicago for most of her life. As a young child, she fell in love with art through illustrated art books by Mike Venzia. Her goal is to make art history accessible to all in ways, such as reforming the canon of art and creating accessible language. She is in her senior year of her bachelor's program in Art History and minoring in Museum and Exhibition Studies at UIC. Her research is focused on making art active and educational through interactive components in museums and homes.

Daniel Tucker works as an artist, writer, educator, and organizer developing documentaries, publications, classes, exhibitions and events inspired by his interest in social movements and the people and places from which they emerge. He works as an Assistant Professor and Graduate Program Director in Socially-Engaged Art at Moore College of Art & Design and his work is documented at miscprojects.com

Nina White is completing a PhD studentship at Middlesbrough Institute of Modern Art, Teesside University, in the North East of England. Nina's thesis is entitled 'The rhizome and the museum: a post-qualitative inquiry into the nature of museums activism at Middlesbrough Institute of Modern Art,' and focuses on knowledge co-production through community programming. Prior to this, Nina completed an MA in Irish Studies at University of Liverpool while working as a Gallery Assistant at Tate Liverpool. Nina she/her pronouns.

Loren Wright is a proud Wisconsinite passionate about telling Black stories in the museum. She received her BA in American Culture Studies from Washington University in St. Louis and her MA in Museum & Exhibition Studies from the University of Illinois Chicago. Her research explores critical fabulation as curatorial praxis.

NOTES

Introduction

1. Amanda Cachia, "The Politics of Creative Access: Guidelines for a Critical Dis/ability Curatorial Practice," in *Interdisciplinary Approaches to Disability* Volume 2, ed. Katie Ellis, Rosemarie Garland-Thomson, Mike Kent, and Rachel Robertson (London/New York: Routledge, 2018), 99–108.

Language In Transit

1. Javairia Shahid, "Language Matters," *Fwd: Museums 2: Small,* (2017): 3.

1. Buy-A-Bus

1. "Buy a Bus," Washington State University, accessed April 21, 2019, https://museum.wsu.edu/education/buy-a-busload-of-kids/.
2. "Program Supporters," Washington State University, accessed April 21, 2019, https://museum.wsu.edu/education/program-supporters/.

2. How We Move

1. Joseph Stromberg, "The Forgotten History Of How Automakers Invented The Crime Of Jaywalking,'" *Vox*, Nov 4, 2015, https://www.vox.com/2015/1/15/7551873/jaywalking-history.
2. Ta-Nehisi Coates, "The Case for Reparations" *The Atlantic*, accessed March 18, 2021, https://www.theatlantic.com/magazine/archive/2014/06/the-case-for-reparations/361631/.
   Another useful resource on the topic is the online Mapping Prejudice project of the University of Minnesota Library: "What Are Covenants?" *University of Minnesota Library*, accessed March 18, 2021, https://mappingprejudice.umn.edu/what-are-covenants/.
3. Mark Di Ionno, "Route 280 Project Looks At Downside Of Highway" *NJ.com*, July 31, 2016, https://www.nj.com/news/

2016/07/route_280_project_looks_at_downside_of_highway_di.ht
ml.

4. Jonathan English,"Why Did America Give Up on Mass Transit? (Don't Blame Cars.)," *Bloomberg City Lab*, August 31, 2018, https://www.bloomberg.com/news/features/2018-08-31/why-is-american-mass-transit-so-bad-it-s-a-long-story.

5. Charles Baudelaire (Jonathan Mayne, trans.), "The Painter of Modern Life (Le Peintre de la Vie Moderne)," *Art in Paris, 1845–1862*. (London: Phaidon Publishers, 1965). Originally published in 1863, this text introduced Baudelaire's invented character of the passionate spectator who wanders, observes and "saunters" the city. The term flâneur was popularized by this text and has since become a recurring reference in art history. Critic Doreen St Felix offers a useful update in her 2016 piece for *Good Magazine*, "The Peril of Black Mobility": https://www.good.is/features/issue-36-flanerie (March 29, 2016).

6. Joseph N. DiStefano,"GoPuff Leaves Busy Philly Site Where Neighbors Railed About Its Traffic," *Philadelphia Inquirer*, November 3, 2020, https://www.inquirer.com/business/gopuff-convenience-store-delievry-beer-center-city-philadelphia-traffic-trucks-complaints-mayor-softbank-drexel-20201103.html.

7. Bob Pool, "Signs Point to West Side Transit Mystery" *Los Angeles Times*, August 16th, 2000.

8. Steve Hymon, "Metro programs that work toward racial justice," June 26, 2020, https://thesource.metro.net/2020/06/26/metro-programs-that-work-toward-racial-justice/.

9. Pool, "Signs Point."

10. Zeiger, Mimi. 2015. "Marmol Radziner's Past Forays into Guerrilla Architecture," *The Architect's Newspaper*, October 29, 2015, https://www.archpaper.com/2015/10/heavy-trash-marmol-radziner-past-forays-guerrilla-architecture/.

11. Heavy Trash,"The Aqua Line," *Heavy Trash*, April 5, 2005, http://heavytrash.blogspot.com/2005/04/aqua-line.html.

12. Michael Manville, "Measure M and the Potential Transformation of Mobility in Los Angeles," *University of California Institute of Transportation Studies*, https://www.its.ucla.edu/wp-content/uploads/sites/6/2019/01/Measure-M-and-the-Potential-Transformation-of-Mobility-in-Los-Angeles.pdf.

13. "Fast Facts 1990–2017 National-Level U.S. Greenhouse Gas Inventory," EPA.gov, April 11, 2019, https://www.epa.gov/sites/production/files/2019-04/documents/2019_fast_facts_508_0.pdf.

14. Ryan Reft, "From Bus Riders Union to Bus Rapid Transit: Race, Class, and Transit Infrastructure in Los Angeles" *KCET.org*, May 14, 2015, https://www.kcet.org/history-society/from-bus-riders-

union-to-bus-rapid-transit-race-class-and-transit-infrastructure-in-los-angeles.

15. Gregory Erhardt, et al., "Do Transportation Network Companies Decrease or Increase Congestion?" *Science Advances*, May 8, 2019, https://advances.sciencemag.org/content/5/5/eaau2670.

16. New York Taxi Workers (@NYTWA), "BREAKING: NYTWA drivers call for one hour work stoppage @ JFK airport today 6 PM to 7 PM to protest #muslimban! #nobannowall" Twitter post, January 28, 2017, https://twitter.com/nytwa/status/825462249468919808.

17. Emma Fitzsimmons, "A Taxi Driver Took His Own Life. His Family Blames Uber's Influence," *New York Times*, May 1, 2018, https://www.nytimes.com/2018/05/01/nyregion/a-taxi-driver-took-his-own-life-his-family-blames-ubers-influence.html.

18. RideShare Drivers United | AUS&USA, http://ridesharedriversunited.com/.

19. Yaseen Aslam and Jamie Woodcock "A History of Uber Organizing in the UK," *South Atlantic Quarterly* 119, no. 2 (2020): 412–421. doi: https://doi.org/10.1215/00382876-8177983.

20. Skip Descant, "2018 Was the Year of the Car, and Transit Ridership Felt It," *Government Tech*, April 30, 2019, https://www.govtech.com/fs/transportation/2018-Was-the-Year-of-the-Car-and-Transit-Ridership-Felt-It.html.

21. Sam Schwartz, "Autonomous Vehicles Are Coming and There's No Roadmap (Yet)," *Next City*, November 26, 2018, https://nextcity.org/features/view/autonomous-vehicles-are-coming-and-theres-no-roadmap-yet.

22. Erica (Erick) Lyle, "The Future of Nowhere" *Streetopia*, ed. Erica Lyle (New York: Booklyn, 2015), 206.

23. Sarah Goodyear, Citylab "The Bike-Share Boom," accessed June 1, 2019, https://web.archive.org/web/20190812024542/https://www.citylab.com/city-makers-connections/bike-share/.

24. Laura Newberry, "Fed-up locals are setting electric scooters on fire and burying them at sea" *Los Angeles Times*, August 20, 2018 https://www.latimes.com/local/lanow/la-me-ln-bird-scooter-vandalism-20180809-story.html.

25. NABSA/North American Bikeshare Association, *Emerging Issue: Dockless Bikeshare in North America*, PDF file, August 31st, 2019, http://nabsa.net/wp-content/uploads/2017/04/StationlessBikeshareMessaging.pdf.

26. Paul Farber, "16: Not Peaceable and Quiet with Counterpublic artists Matt Joynt, Anthony Romero, and Josh Rios." May 24th, 2019, *Monument Lab*, Recorded live at the Pulitzer Art Foundation, podcast, 54:14, https://monumentlab.com/podcast/not-

peaceable-and-quiet-with-counterpublic-artists-matt-joynt-anthony-romero-and-josh-rios.

27. Josh Rios, phone interview with the author, April 16th, 2021.

28. Rachel Handler, "What the Hole Is Going On? The Very Real, Totally Bizarre Bucatini Shortage of 2020," *Grub Street*, December 28, 2020, https://www.grubstreet.com/2020/12/2020-bucatini-shortage-investigation.html.

29. Gutelius, Beth "Global Production Networks from Below: Geographies of Labor in Logistics" PhD Diss (University of Illinois at Chicago, 2016) p. 97, https://indigo.uic.edu/articles/thesis/Global_Production_Networks_from_Below_Geographies_of_Labor_in_Logistics/10889396/1.

30. Shannon Mattern, "Infrastructural Tourism" *Places Journal*, July, 2013, https://placesjournal.org/article/infrastructural-tourism.

31. Guy Debord, "Theory of the Dérive" *Lèvres Nues*, 9 (1956) reprinted in *Internationale Situationniste*, 2 (1958), https://www.cddc.vt.edu/sionline/si/theory.html. Compass took inspiration from the French Situationists, the group to which Debord belonged, and their practice of the *dérive* (*drift* in English) for their "drifts" in the American midwest.

32. Claire Pentecost and Brian Holmes, "Continental Drift Then and Now: Update on a Decade-Long Experiment," Lecture, Museum of Modern Art in Warsaw, 2016, https://vimeo.com/168770654.

33. Rozalinda Borcila and Brian Holmes, "The FTZ Device" *Southwest Corridor Northwest Passage*, accessed March 30, 2021, https://web.archive.org/web/20170630175740/http://southwestcorridornorthwestpassage.org/the-ftz-as-device/.

34. Rozalinda Borcila, "Riding the Zone," *Deep Routes: The Midwest in All Directions*, ed. Rozalinda Borcila, Bonnie Fortune and Sarah Ross, (Chicago: Compass Collaborators, 2012), 149.

35. Rozalinda Borcila, "Riding the Zone," *Deep Routes: The Midwest in All Directions*, ed. Rozalinda Borcila, Bonnie Fortune and Sarah Ross, (Chicago: Compass Collaborators, 2012), 154.

3. Visualizing Loss at the Oriental Institute Museum

1. I chose to use the phrase "Middle Eastern" here, because it is an accessible term that encompasses all of the geographic areas represented in the OI's holdings and evokes contemporary issues, but it is a modern socio-political classification that describes the region from a Euro-American reference point—and a designation that many 'Middle Eastern' people and governments may object to. Conversely, the Oriental Institute describes itself as a center for the

study of "ancient Near Eastern" civilizations. Steeped in academia and imperialism, the term 'Near Eastern' and the name 'Oriental Institute' not only center the Euro-American perspective but also emerge from a colonialist attitude toward the region, its objects, and its cultures. This footnote reflects an ongoing and controversial discussion among many institutions including the Oriental Institute, but it is reasonable to assert that no single term can adequately describe all of the countries, cultures, and geographic areas included in this diverse region in either its ancient or modern contexts.

2. "Contemporary Art Installations," *Oriental Institute*, accessed March 15, 2020, https://oi100.uchicago.edu/contemporary-art.

3. Michael Rakowitz, *The invisible enemy should not exist*, drawings, Arabic newspaper and food packaging cardboard sculptures, museum labels, sound, 2007–Ongoing, http://www.michaelrakowitz.com/the-invisible-enemy-should-not-exist.

4. Jack Wang, "Artist reimagines ancient Middle Eastern artifact in vivid color," *UChicago News*, October 2, 2019, https://news.uchicago.edu/story/artist-reimagines-ancient-middle-eastern-artifact-vivid-color.

5. Omar Kholeif, Ella Shohat, Shumon Basar, and Michael Rakowitz, *Michael Rakowitz: Backstroke of the West.* (Chicago: Museum of Contemporary Art Chicago, 2017), 43. While I in no way intend to minimize the devastating impact of looting and the antiquities trade, I point out this difference to emphasize the permanence of violent destruction.

6. Wang, "Artist reimagines."

7. There is an irony in Rakowitz's use of color. It sharply contrasts the surrounding items, which are monotone and weathered. The comparison makes Rakowitz's intervention seem dynamic, vibrant, and lively while the ancient objects are muted, quiet, and almost fade into the background. We are used to seeing ancient artifacts in this way, but evidence suggests that the original Neo-Assyrian reliefs were also brightly colored. Though Rakowitz's work diverges from the visitor's expectations of antiquity, the reappearance is, in a way, more truthful to the lost object.

8. Marcia Biggs. "Reduced to Rubble by ISIS, Archaeologists See a New Day for Ancient City of Nimrud," *PBS News Hour*, podcast, transcript, April 12, 2017, https://www.pbs.org/newshour/show/reduced-rubble-isis-archaeologists-see-new-day-ancient-city-nimrud.

9. Lucy Kafanov. "Iraqis Mourn Destruction of Ancient City of Nimrud: ISIS 'Tried to Destroy the Identity of Iraq.'" *NBC News*, December 11, 2016, https://www.nbcnews.com/storyline/isis-

terror/iraqis-mourn-destruction-ancient-city-nimrud-isis-tried-destroy-identity-n694636.

10. "'The Invisible Enemy Should Not Exist', Michael Rakowitz, 2007-Ongoing," *The Tate Modern*, accessed January 5, 2021, https://www.tate.org.uk/art/artworks/rakowitz-the-invisible-enemy-should-not-exist-t15347.

11. Rakowitz et al, *Backstroke of the West*, 12.

12. Object label, *Reappearance of Panel G-13*, Oriental Institute Museum, Chicago, IL.

13. Wang, "Artist reimagines."

14. Yesomi Umolu, "On Limits of Care and Knowledge: 15 Points Museums Must Understand to Dismantle Structural Injustice." *Artnet News*, June 25, 2020, https://news.artnet.com/opinion/limits-of-care-and-knowledge-yesomi-umolu-op-ed-1889739.

15. Emily Teeter, "A History of the OI Museum," In *Discovering New Pasts: The OI at 100* (Chicago: The Oriental Institute 2019), 62, https://oi.uchicago.edu/sites/oi.uchicago.edu/files/uploads/shared/docs/Publications/Misc/miscdiscoveringnewpasts.pdf.

16. Teeter, "A History of the OI Museum," 68.

17. James Henry Breasted. *The University of Chicago Survey Volume XII* (Chicago: The University of Chicago Press, 1933), ix. https://oi.uchicago.edu/sites/oi.uchicago.edu/files/uploads/shared/docs/The_Oriental_Institute_Breasted.pdf.

18. Breasted, *Chicago Survey*, 2.

19. In terms of its research, collection, and curation, many nuanced approaches to the museum have, of course, been enacted in the 100 years since the Oriental Institute was created, but these founding events and attitudes leave their mark on the institution today. They must be reckoned with.

20. The Penn Museum's Global Guides program and Ahmed Badr's Narratio Fellowship, a collaboration with the Met, are examples of these efforts.

6. In Transition

1. Controversy around migration has also been represented by museological responses to the travel ban (in February 2017) in New York City by The Museum of Modern Art and The Metropolitan Museum of Art. See: Melissa Forstrom, "Innovation in Interpretation: Museological Responses to the Travel Ban," in *Museum Innovation: Building More Equitable, Relevant and Impactful Museums,* eds. Haitham Eid and Melissa Forstrom (New York: Routledge, [forthcoming] 2021). For a discussion about MoMA's response see: Maria Vlachou, "Dividing Issues and Mission-Driven Activism," in

Museum Activism, eds. Robert R. Janes, R.R. and Richard Sandell (New York: Routledge, 2019), 47–57. And: Dina A. Bailey, "The activist spectrum in United States museums," in *Museum Activism*, eds. Robert R. Janes, R.R. and Richard Sandell (New York: Routledge, 2019), 293–303.

For documentation of exhibitions that represent migration, see: Anna Chiara Cimoli and Maria Vlachou, *Museums and Migration* website, accessed December 28, 2020, https://museumsandmigration.wordpress.com. This website does not document either exhibition discussed in this article.

2. Looking ahead and for the purposes of this paper, the term "migration" is inclusive of the three types of migration. The European Commission defines migration as: "In the global context, movement of a person either across an international border (international migration), or within a state (internal migration) for more than one year irrespective of the causes, voluntary or involuntary, and the means, regular or irregular, used to migrate"; and a forced migrant is defined as: A person subject to a migratory movement in which an element of coercion exists, including threats to life and livelihood, whether arising from natural or man-made causes."Migration and Home Affairs," European Commission, accessed March 3, 2021, https://ec.europa.eu/home-affairs/index_en.

Using the 1951 Geneva Convention, the UN Refugee agency, (UNHCR) defines refugee as: "someone who is unable or unwilling to return to their country of origin owing to a well-founded fear of being persecuted for reason of race, religion, nationality, membership of a particular social group, or political opinion." "What is a refugee?," *UNHCR*, accessed March 14, 2021, https://www.unhcr.org/en-us/what-is-a-refugee.html.

3. The June 21, 2020 was the intended exhibition closing date. In reality, the quarantine relating to the novel coronavirus, Covid-19 closed the exhibition in March 2020.

4. Carol Duncan, *Civilizing Rituals: Inside Public Art Museum* (New York: Routledge, 1995), 19.

5. Lynda Kelly and Fiona Cameron, *Hot Topics, Public Culture, Museums* (Cambridge: Cambridge Scholars Publishing, 2010), 3.

6. Forstrom, "Innovation in Interpretation: Museological Responses to the Travel Ban."

7. Kelly and Cameron, *Hot Topics, Public Culture, Museums*, 1–2.

8. Robert R. Janes and Richard Sandell, "Posterity has arrived: The necessary emergence of museum activism," in *Museum Activism*, eds. Robert R. Janes and Richard Sandell (New York: Routledge, 2019), 1–22.

9. Kelly and Cameron, *Hot Topics, Public Culture, Museums*, 1.

10. Janes and Sandell, "Posterity has arrived: The necessary emergence of museum activism," 15.
11. Laurence Gouriévidis, "Representing Migration in Museums: History, diversity and the politics of memory," in *Museums and Migration: History, Memory, Politics*, ed. Laurence Gouriévidis (New York: Routledge, 2014), 9.
12. Richard Sandell, *Museums, Society, Inequality* (Abingdon: Routledge, 2002).
13. It is important to note that migration is a theme of numerous artworks exhibited in both exhibitions, however, due to space limitations, this is not discussed in this article.
14. A special thank you to both Brinda Kumar and Meredith Brown, for taking the time to speak with me about this exhibition in October 2020.
15. The Met announced in June 2020 that it would not reopen the Breuer location after the pandemic.
16. Ayşin Yoltar-Yildirim "Behind an Exhibition at the Brooklyn Museum: 'Syria, Then and Now: Stories from Refugees a Century Apart," *Forced Migration and Cultural Production, Cultural Policy Yearbook 2019*, accessed December 28, 2020, https://iletisim.com.tr/dergiler/kultur-politikasi-yillik/5/sayi-2-cultural-policy-yearbook-2019/10044/behind-an-exhibition-at-the-brooklyn-museum-syria-then-and-now-stories-from-refugees-a-century-apart/11815.
17. *Ibid.*
18. Some of the changes at the Brooklyn Museum since Director Anne Pasternak's tenure beginning in 2015, include the moving of the gift shop to the glass façade (2004) in almost the exact space that August Rodin's "The Burghers of Calais (1889) sculptures used to occupy, which could be viewed by the general public because of their placement. For a discussion that includes this example at the Brooklyn Museum (before the move of the sculptures), see: Peter Ride, "Suspended: Art in the Threshold," in *Museum Thresholds: The Design and Media of Arrival*, eds. Ross Parry, Ruth Page and Alex Moseley (New York: Routledge, 2018), 81–106.
19. "Syria emergency", *UNHCR*, accessed March 14, 2021, https://www.unhcr.org/en-us/syria-emergency.html.
20. Adapted from: Melissa Forstrom, "Interpretative Responses: NYC Museums and the Muslim Travel Ban" Presentation, University of the Arctic, Tromsø, Norway, September 18, 2018.
21. See: Paulette McManus, "Oh, Yes, They Do: How Museum Visitors Read Labels and Interact with Exhibit Texts," *Curator* 32 no. 3 (1989): 186. And: Forstrom, "Innovation in Interpretation: Museological Responses to the Travel Ban."
22. Forstrom, "Innovation in Interpretation: Museological Responses to the Travel Ban."

23. Louise Ravelli, *Museum Texts: Communication Frameworks*, Museum Meanings Series (New York: Routledge, 2006), 2–5.

24. Erving Goffman, *Frame Analysis: An Essay on the Organization of Experience* (Boston: Northeastern University Press, 1986).

25. Todd Gitlin, *The Whole World is Watching: Mass Media in the Making and Unmaking of the New Left* (Berkeley: University of California Press, 1980), 7.

26. Christopher Whitehead, *Interpreting Art in Museums and Galleries*, (New York: Routledge, 2012), 53.

27. Arguably there are messages and interpretation everywhere in museums—from the entry narrative, through the space of the exhibition and design communication—all of which have meaning and convey messages to audiences. See: Melissa Forstrom "Interpretation and Visitors in Two Islamic Art Exhibitions PhD diss., (University of Westminster, 2017); Christopher Whitehead, *Interpreting Art in Museums and Galleries* (New York: Routledge, 2012); and Louise Ravelli, *Museum Texts: Communication Frameworks* (New York: Routledge, 2006). However, due to the space limitations of this paper and the explicitness of written interpretation, this argument is limited to written interpretation.

28. Meredith Brown and Brinda Kumar, interview with author, Zoom call, October 14, 2020.

29. The full introduction text of *Home Is a Foreign Place* reads:

   Contemporary art and earlier avant-garde movements of modern art do not have a single origin, nor do they develop in isolation. Since the 1940s, artists have sought new forms of expression as they have lived through culturally transformative events, from devastating wars, social and humanitarian injustices, and mass migration to economic and environmental change. These histories continue to impact and inform the art of our time. In the following galleries works are united by shared engagements with language, architecture, space and politics that demonstrate the movement of ideas and identities across cultural and national boundaries. The resulting visual conversations emphasize the significance of parallel artistic impulses in the world and over time, while remaining attentive to the specific local and historical circumstances of their making.

   "Home Is a Foreign Place" highlights recent acquisitions of modern and contemporary art from Latin America, the Middle East, North Africa, and South and Southeast Asia, alongside works by iconic American artists from The Met collection. Taking its title from Zarina's 199 suite of thirty-six woodcuts, on view nearby, this collection display features art that explores the meanings of finding a "home" and "place" in our increasingly interwoven globe, whether by necessity or choice.

30. The full introduction text of *Syria, Then and Now* reads:

   Syria: At the turn of the twentieth century, Syria gave shelter to refugees arriving from Russian-ethnic Circassians, who had been displaced by the Russian conquest of the Caucasus in the nineteenth century. But today, in contrast, a new generation of refugees seeks to escape Syrian itself, after the regime of Bashar al-Assad used violence to put down pro-democracy protests in 2011 and civil war broke out, plunging the country into turmoil. As these changing tides of history suggest, anyone, anywhere, can become a refugee, and no geographical location can guarantee immunity.

Then: This exhibition presents a group of ceramics found in Raqqa, Syria by Circassian refuges around the turn of the twentieth century. When Circassians came to Raqqa, they searched for bricks to build houses. In the process, they unearth not only the masonry of Raqqa's once magnificent medieval Islamic architecture but also its ceramics, buried since the thirteenth century, when the city was destroyed by invading Mongol armies.

Now: In our day, Raqqa has become synonymous with ISIS, the terrorist group which until recently proclaimed a new Islamic caliphate from the same town that the eighth-century Islamic leader Caliph Harum al-Rashid once rules his Abbasid empire. The ravages of ISIS and the ongoing civil war, amid continuing acts of violence against civilians, forced many to seek refuge outside Syria, not only in neighboring countries, but also in distant lands, in Europe and North America. Their plight is the shared concern of three contemporary artists, representing three generations born, respectively in the 1940s, 1960s, and 1980s: Ginane Makki Bacho, Issam Kourbaj, and Mohamad Hafez. Each of them tells a different story, but in the end, each calls upon our common humanity for compassionate attention to refugees' precarious situation worldwide.

31. Vlachou "Dividing Issues and Mission-Driven Activism: Museum responses to migration policies and the refugee crisis," 47.
32. Gouriévidis, "Representing Migration in Museums: History, diversity and the politics of memory," 1.
33. Two important exceptions are: Research Field 4 of the MeLA project (European Museums in an age of migrations. Research Field 4: Curatorial and Artistic Research, "examined how the relationship between art, migration and representation is being addressed in contemporary artistic and curatorial practices, and what question this raised for artists, curators, and audiences." However, there is a focus on the relationship between curator and living artist in contemporary art museums. And Andrew Dewdney, David Dibosa, and Victoria Walsh, *Post Critical Museology, Theory and Practice in the Art Museum*, (New York: Routledge, 2013). This book details a research project with Tate Museums group, called Tate Encounters in the United Kingdom, which involved research with twelve students for a two-year period where the criteria for participation was "[…] that the students should be the first in their immediate family to attend higher education and that either they, their parents or grandparents has migrated [to the UK]," 16. Importantly, all of this research outlined above was conducted before the precipitous rise of right-wing nationalism in many European coun-

tries and the inflammatory Trump presidency (2017-2021), which arguably marginalized and vilified immigrants/migrants.

34. Kelly and Cameron, *Hot Topics, Public Culture, Museums*, 1.

35. See: Multaka: Museum as Meeting Point project in Berlin museums: https://multaka.de/en/project-2/. And the announcement that the Louvre would undertake a similar project, funded by the Saudi, Alwaleed Philanthropies. See https://www.theartnewspaper.com/news/louvre-planning-a-multaka-programme-for-refugee-communities.

36. See: Dina A. Bailey, "The activist spectrum in United States museums," in *Museum Activism*, eds. Robert R. Janes, R.R. and Richard Sandell (New York: Routledge, 2019), 293–303 and Vlachou "Dividing Issues and Mission-Driven Activism: Museum responses to migration policies and the refugee crisis," 47–57.

37. I use the term "rapid response interpreting" to describe both The Met and MoMA's response to the 2017 travel ban, which is defined as the social innovation, development, and communication of oral and/written interpretation that responds, intervenes and addresses contemporary socio-politics contemporaneously in museum spaces with the intention of creating and revealing the relevancy of museum objects to contemporary life, in: "Innovation in Interpretation: Museological Responses to the Travel Ban."

38. At the V&A, "Refugee Flag" was exhibited in Gallery 21, at the intersection of the new Sackler Courtyard/Blavanik Hall (2017), the tunnel entrance, and the original "South Kensington Museum" building (1857) as part of the "Rapid Response Collecting" initiative. At MoMA, "Refugee Flag" was exhibited in the public Garden Lobby before the closing for renovations in June 2019.

39. Ayşin Yoltar-Yildirim, "Behind an Exhibition at the Brooklyn Museum."

40. Christopher Whitehead et al., "Place, Identity and Migration and European Museums," in *Museums, Migration and Identity in Europe: People, Places and Identities*, eds. Christopher Whitehead et al. (New York: Routledge, 2015), 7–8.

41. Ruth Noack, "A small number of useful contributions towards building an argument about the role of museums in a migratory society that take into account artistic practices, collections, exhibitions-and audience-making," in *Agency, Ambivalence, Analysis: Approaching the Museum with Migration in Mind*, MeLA Books 06-04, ed. Ruth Noack (Milan, Italy: Politecnico di Milano, March 2013): 15, http://www.mela-project.polimi.it/upl/cms/attach/20130708/172725825_1912.pdf.

42. Ruth Noack, "A small number of useful contributions," 15.

43. As discussed by: Noack, "A small number of useful contributions," 15.

44. Marzia Varutti, "Towards social inclusion in Taiwan: museums, equality and indigenous groups," in *Museums, Equality and Social Justice*, eds. Richard Sandell and Eithne Nightingale (New York: Routledge, 2012), 243–253.
45. Gouriévidis, "Representing Migration in Museums: History, diversity and the politics of memory," 11.

7. Responding to Activism

1. Joshua G. Adair and Amy K. Levin, eds., *Museums, Sexuality, and Gender Activism* (London: Routledge, 2020). Adair served as editorial assistant for the first book.
2. *Museums Are Not Neutral*, accessed January 12, 2021, https://www.museumsarenotneutral.com.
3. Aleia Brown, "The Confederate Flag Does Not Belong in a Museum," *Slate*, June 25, 2015, https://slate.com/news-and-politics/2015/06/confederate-flag-it-doesnt-belong-at-the-south-carolina-capitol-it-doesnt-belong-in-a-museum-either.html.
4. *Decolonize This Place*, accessed January 12, 2021, https://decolonizethisplace.org.
5. Regan de Loggans, "Mistikôsiwak: Monkman at the Met," *Canadian Art*, April 29, 2020, https://canadianart.ca/essays/mistikosiwak-kent-monkman-at-the-met/.
6. "Toolkit," Museums As a Site for Social Action, accessed January 12, 2021, https://static1.squarespace.com/static/58fa685dff7c50f78be5f2b2/t/59dcdd27e5dd5b5a1b51d9d8/1507646780650/TOOLKIT_10_2017.pdf.
7. Mirjam Sneeuwloper, Amy K. Levin, Colline Hoorstink, and Yvo Manuel Vas Dias, "Never a Small Project: Welcoming Transgender Communities into the Museum," 268. Regardless of a person's stage in transition, it is best practice to refer to a trans person as their gender they are, not the gender they were assigned at birth.
8. Camille Georgeson-Usher, "All That Moves Us: Bodies in Land," 149.
9. Michael Petry, "On Gender Fluidity and Photographic Portraiture," 256.

8. Grasping at Relevancy

1. Jeffrey Chapline and Juline K. Johnson, *The National Endowment for the Arts Guide to Community-Engaged Research in the Arts and Health* (Washington, D.C.: National Endowment for the Arts Office of Research & Analysis, 2016); Helen Chatterjee and Guy Noble,

Museums, Health, and Well-Being (London: Routledge, 2017); Sarah Desmarias, Laura Bedford, and Helen Chatterjee, *Museums as Spaces of Well-being: A Second Report from the National Alliance for Museums, Health, and Wellbeing*, Museums and Well-being Alliance (London: Arts Council England, 2018); Jocelyn Dodd and Ceri Jones, *Mind, Body, Spirit: How Museums Impact Health and Well-being* (Leicester: Research Centre for Museums and Galleries, School of Museum Studies, University of Leicester, 2014); Adam Rozan, "Museums at 2040," *Museums* 96, no. 6 (2017): 17-21; Lois Silverman, *The Social Work of Museums* (London: Routledge, 2010).

2. Brenda Cowan, Ross Laird, and Jason McKeown, *Museum Objects, Health and Healing: The Relationship between Exhibitions and Wellness* (London: Routledge, 2019); Zachary Small, "Museums Embrace Art Therapy Techniques for Unsettled Times," *The New York Times*, June 15, 2020, https://www.nytimes.com/2020/06/15/arts/design/art-therapy-museums-virus.html.

3. Jackie Armstrong, "Museums Must Become More Trauma Informed," *Art Museum Teaching* (blog), August 3, 2020, https://artmuseumteaching.com/2020/08/03/museums-must-become-more-trauma-informed/; Dina Bailey, "We Can't Go Back to Normal: Responding to Trauma Within the Museum Field," *Viewfinder: Reflecting in Museum Education* 11, September 11, 2020, https://medium.com/viewfinder-reflecting-on-museum-education/we-cant-go-back-to-normal-responding-to-trauma-within-the-museum-field-3f924152850e.

4. Rozan, 'Museums at 2040,' *Museum*, 26.

5. Brian Hogarth, "Code Red for the Museum Education Profession," *Art Museum Teaching* (blog), May 6, 2020, https://artmuseumteaching.com/2020/05/06/code-red/.

6. Mara Naiditch, Rachel Gertz, and Edgar Chamorro, "How Do You Museum?: Marketing User-Generated Content to Engage Audiences" (paper presentation, Museums and the Web 2017, Cleveland, OH, April 20, 2017); P. B. Jarreau, N. S. Dahmen, and E. Jones, "Instagram and the Science Museum: a Missed Opportunity for Public Engagement," *Journal of Science Communication* 18, no. 02 (2019), https://doi.org/10.22323/2.18020206.

7. Helen Holmes, "Closed to Visitors, Museums Are Finding Their Community Outreach More Necessary Than Ever," *Observer*, March 20, 2020, https://observer.com/2020/03/museums-virtual-programming-coronavirus-community-engagement/.

8. Joan Baldwin, "Museum Access in the Age of COVID and Beyond," *Leadership Matters* (blog), May 4, 2020, https://leadershipmatters1213.wordpress.com/2020/05/04/museum-access-in-the-age-of-covid-and-beyond/.

9. Casey D. Mull and Katherine Rose Adams, "The Identification, Influence, and Impact of Boundary Spanners Within Research-Practice Partnerships," in *Exploring the Community Impact of Research-Practice Partnerships in Education*, ed. R. Martin Reardon and Jack Leonard (Charlotte: Information Age Publishing, Inc., 2017), 271–297.

10. Laxmi Parthasarathy and Cristi Hegranes, "Leading a Global Team Through Crisis Means Focusing on Local Details," *Stanford Social Innovation Review* (blog), May 18, 2020, https://ssir.org/articles/ entry/leading_a_global_team_through_crisis_means_focusing_on_ local_details.

11. For recent panel discussions highlighting virtual education programs, see Erin Branham, Tara Burns, Valentina Quezada, and Sarah Wilson, "#MESCommunity: The Future of K-12 Field Trips, Part 2" (virtual panel discussion, Museum Educators of Southern California, January 25, 2021); Zoe Silverman, Lindsay Kranz, Grace VanderVliet, Cynthia Dearborn, Olivia Morgan, Claire Schultz, Sadie Helmick, and Juline Chevalier, "Celebrate the Wins" (virtual ignite talk, National Art Education Association Museum Education Division Preconference, February 25, 2021); Theresa Sotto, Tara Burns, Hallie Scott, Adjoa Jones de Almeida, Raul Baltazar, Vashti Dubois and OnRaé LaTeal Watkins, "Reimagining the Museum: Community, Collaboration & Radical Inclusion" (virtual panel discussion, Hammer Museum, Los Angeles, CA, March 24, 2021).

12. *Museum Workers Relief Fund: A Museum Workers Speak Initiative*, March 20, 2021, https://sites.google.com/view/museumworkersspeak.

13. Change the Museum, *Instagram*, March 29, 2021, https://www. instagram.com/changethemuseum.

14. *Death to Museums* archive, https://www.youtube.com/ channel/UCiLyLYvXIWghzWezCjZEJXQ.

15. Dan Hicks, Victor Ehikhamenor, Lauren Kroiz, Natasha Becker, and Marla Berns, "The British Museums: Benin Bronzes, Colonial Violence, Cultural Restitution" (virtual panel discussion, Phoebe A. Hearst Museum of Anthropology, February 12, 2021).

16. Johnnetta B. Cole, Lonnie G. Bunch III, and Lori Foggarty, "Racism, Unrest, and the Role of the Museum Field" (virtual panel discussion, American Alliance of Museums Annual Meeting, June 3, 2020).

17. Adam Popescu, "How Will We Remember the Pandemic? Museums Are Already Deciding," *The New York Times*, May 25, 2020, https://www.nytimes.com/2020/05/25/arts/design/ museums-covid-19-collectinghtml.

9. The Mess of the Canon

1. Zdenka Badovinac, *Comradeship: Curating, Art, and Politics in Post-socialist Europe* (New York, Independent Curators International: 2019).

2. Master narrative here is directly linked and derived from Modernity, which emerges and develops as the culture of the bourgeois, with its origins marked with the separation between Christian worldviews and the autonomy of institutions of science, law, and art. The modernist master narrative is one of *one* truth, *one* method, *one* system, and *one* ideology, which was to create *one* 'new' world of art. Badovinac is precisely challenging this unilateral ideology.

3. Badovinac, *Comradeship*, 22.

4. Badovinac, *Comradeship*, 29.

5. André Malraux (1901–1976) was a French novelist, art historian, and statesman best known for his trilogy: *The Psychology of Art* (1947–1950), *The Voices of Silence* (1951), *Museum Without Walls* (1952–1954), and *The Metamorphosis of the Gods* (1957–1976). Walter Benjamin (1892–1940) was a German literary critic and essayist and among his best known works are the essays "The Task of the Translator" (1923), "The Work of Art in the Age of Mechanical Reproduction" (1935), and "Theses on the Philosophy of History" (1940).

6. Badovinac, *Comradeship*, 127.

7. Badovinac, *Comradeship*, 11.

8. Badovinac, *Comradeship*, 36.

9. Badovinac, *Comradeship*, 68.

10. Badovinac, *Comradeship*, 119.

11. In 2016, eight years after Badovinac's essays on this topic, the Museum of Modern Art in New York opened the exhibition *Transmissions: Art in Eastern Europe and Latin America, 1960–1980*, which invoked some of the ideas from Badvovinac's writings and served as a much-needed international exhibition grappling with the "true history" of two regions with much in common. *Transmissions: Art in Eastern Europe and Latin America, 1960–1980* was an exhibition at the Museum of Modern Art New York that took place on September 5, 2015 to January 3, 2016 and focused on parallels and connections among artists active in Latin America and Eastern Europe in the 1960s and 1970s. For more information: https://www.moma.org/calendar/exhibitions/1532.

12. Restany also visited Latin America multiple times, participating in juries, writing about young artists, and supporting conceptual and pop art from the region.

13. In the late 1980s and 1990s, there were several international surveys of Latin American art: take for example the exhibition

Latin America: The Modern Era, 1820–1980 that took place in *1989 Hayward Gallery in London* curated by Dawn Ades and *Latin American Artists of the Twentieth Century* that took place in 1993 at the Museum of Modern Art, New York, curated by Waldo Rasmussen.

11. Online Museums: an Opportunity for Access?

1. Schweibenz, Werner. *The 'Virtual Museum': New Perspectives For Museums to Present Objects and Information Using the Internet as a Knowledge Base and Communication System.* PDF File. November 7, 1998, http://www.informationswissenschaft.org/wp-content/uploads/isi/isi1998/14_isi-98-dv-schweibenz-saarbruecken.pdf.
2. "Expanding Your Market: Maintaining Accessibility in Museums," *ADA.gov*, accessed December 13, 2019, https://www.ada.gov/business/museum_access.htm.
3. Amanda Cachia, "The Politics of Creative Access: Guidelines for a Critical Dis/ability Curatorial Practice," in *Interdisciplinary Approaches to Disability Volume 2* (New York: Routledge, 2019), 141.
4. Amanda Cachia, "Talking Blind: Disability, Access, and the Discursive Turn," *Disability Studies Quarterly* 33, no. 3 (2013):15, https://dsq-sds.org/article/view/3758.
5. Patty Berne, "What is Disability Justice?," *Sins Invalid* (blog), June 16, 2020, https://www.sinsinvalid.org/news-1/2020/6/16/what-is-disability-justice.
6. Nomy Lamm, "This is Disability Justice," *The Body Is Not An Apology*, September 2, 2015, https://thebodyisnotanapology.com/magazine/this-is-disability-justice/.
7. Lamm, "This is Disability Justice."
8. *Ibid.*
9. James I. Charlton, *Nothing About Us Without Us* (Berkeley: University of California Press, 1998), traces the historic use of the phrase "nothing about us without us" in the disability rights movement.
10. Emily Watlington. "How To Make Exhibitions And Art Events Accessible," *Art in America*, July 23, 2020, https://www.artnews.com/list/art-in-america/features/ada-compliance-access-art-exhibitions-events-1202695169.
11. Here are some examples of ways that accessibility can be practiced on numerous platforms.For social media accessibility, look at posts by Alice Wong on instagram at the website https://www.instagram.com/alicatsamurai/. The posts include image descriptions and alt text. The Museum of Contemporary Art Chicago website uses the program Coyote that allows visitors to turn on and off image descriptions of photographs and works of art. To see more, go to their website at https://mcachicago.org/.

12. Capital "B" signifies a Blind cultural identity. Lowercase 'b' signifies the medical aspects of blindness.

12. Treading Water: Shallow Analysis in Adrian Franklin's Anti-Museum

1. Adrian Franklin, *Anti-Museum* (New York: Routledge, 2020), 6.
2. Franklin, 9.
3. Franklin, 5.
4. Locations are as follows: Collection de l'Art Brut (Lausanne, Switzerland), Marfa (Texas, United States), PS1 (New York City, United States), the New Museum (New York City, United States), Museum of Old and New Art, or Mona (Tasmania, Australia), and Art42 (Paris, France).
5. Franklin, 69.
6. Franklin, 43–44.
7. Franklin, 101.
8. Adrian Franklin and Nikos Papastergiadis, "Engaging with the Anti-Museum? Visitors to the Museum of Old and New Art," *Journal of Sociology* 53, no. 3 (2017): 9-10. Article cited in Adrian Franklin, *Anti-Museum*, 101.
9. To make my own position clear, I am a queer Black woman, and my identity definitely shapes my understanding of museums and how I hope that they will change. As such, I entered my reading of *Anti-Museum* with expectations that were not met, and they are expectations that another reader may not share.

13. Play Happens Here

1. Abigail Hackett, Rachel Holmes, and Christina MacRae, eds., *Working with Young Children in Museums: Weaving Theory and Practice* (Oxford: Routledge, 2020).
2. Rachel Holmes, Christina MacRae and Abigail Hackett, "Introduction to Part I" in *Working with Young Children in Museums: Weaving Theory and Practice*, eds. Abigail Hackett, Rachel Holmes, and Christina MacRae (Oxford: Routledge, 2020), 17.
3. Lisa Howarth, "The Thing-ness of Wood Chips," in *Working with Young Children in Museums: Weaving Theory and Practice*, eds. Abigail Hackett, Rachel Holmes, and Christina MacRae (Oxford: Routledge, 2020), 37.
4. Abigail Hackett, Rachel Holmes and Christina MacRae, "Introduction I," 8.

5. Abigail Hackett, Rachel Holmes and Christina MacRae, "Introduction I," 9.

6. Abigail Hackett, Rachel Holmes and Christina MacRae, "Introduction to Part II,"in *Working with Young Children in Museums: Weaving Theory and Practice*, eds. Abigail Hackett, Rachel Holmes, and Christina MacRae (Oxford: Routledge, 2020), 77.

7. Kate Noble and Nicola Wallis "Leaving Room for Learning: University of Cambridge Museums' Nursery in Residence," in *Working with Young Children in Museums: Weaving Theory and Practice*, eds. Abigail Hackett, Rachel Holmes, and Christina MacRae (Oxford: Routledge, 2020), 91.

8. Kate Noble and Nicola Wallis "Leaving Room for Learning," 91–92.

9. Kate Noble and Nicola Wallis "Leaving Room for Learning," 93.

10. As an American (even one living in a city), I had to consciously remind myself that many European cities are more walkable and have better infrastructure than in the United States. In Richmond, for example, most museums are accessible via bus. Surrounding counties, however, have (arguably purposeful) fewer bus routes and less access to the city by public transportation.

11. Joanne Drum "Working Off-Site with Families," in *Working with Young Children in Museums: Weaving Theory and Practice*, eds. Abigail Hackett, Rachel Holmes, and Christina MacRae (Oxford: Routledge, 2020), 152.

12. Katy McCall, "Healthy Child Drop-In and Baby Stay and Play at Manchester Art Gallery," in *Working with Young Children in Museums: Weaving Theory and Practice*, eds. Abigail Hackett, Rachel Holmes, and Christina MacRae (Oxford: Routledge, 2020), 166.

13. Katy McCall, "*Healthy Child Drop-In*," 168.

14. Katy McCall, "*Healthy Child Drop-In*,"171.

15. Katy McCall, "*Healthy Child Drop-In*,"172.

16. Katharine Hoare and Kate Kelland, "The Sound of Little Feet at the British Museum," in *Working with Young Children in Museums: Weaving Theory and Practice*, eds. Abigail Hackett, Rachel Holmes, and Christina MacRae (Oxford: Routledge, 2020), 97.

17. In August of 2020, the British Museum released a Collecting and Empire Trail self-guided tour, which takes visitors through the complex histories of some of their collections. There does not seem to be a child-friendly version.

18. American Alliance of Museums, "United States May Lose One-third of All Museums, New Survey Shows," *American Alliance of Museums*, July 22, 2020, https://www.aam-us.org/2020/07/22/united-states-may-lose-one-third-of-all-museums-new-survey-shows/.

19. Alex Thorp, "On What Grounds," in *Working with Young Children in Museums: Weaving Theory and Practice*, eds. Abigail Hackett, Rachel Holmes, and Christina MacRae (Oxford: Routledge, 2020), 188.

14. Debunk, Decenter, and Diversify

1. Roy Rosenzweig and David Thelen, *The Presence of the Past: Popular Uses of History in American Life* (New York: Columbia University Press, 1998), 21–22.
2. Hilary Iris Lowe, "Dwelling in Possibility," *The Public Historian* 37, no. 2 (2015): 46.
3. Peter B. Meyer, "The Airplane as an Open-Source Invention," *Revue économique* 64, no. 1 (2013): 125–126.
4. Tom Crouch, *A Dream of Wings: Americans and the Airplane, 1875–1905* (New York: Norton, 2002), 296; Orville Wright, *How We Made the First Flight* (Washington, DC: Federal Aviation Administration Office of Public Affairs, 1986).
5. Ruth Graham, "The great historic house museum debate," *Boston Globe*, August 10, 2014, https://www.bostonglobe.com/ideas/ 2014/08/09/the-great-historic-house-museum-debate/ jzFwE9tvJdHDCXehIWqK4O/story.html; Ron M. Potvin, "House or Home? Rethinking the House Museum Paradigm," *History News* (2010): 9–11; Richard Moe, "Are There Too Many House Museums?," *Forum Journal* 27, no. 1 (2012): 55–61.
6. Callie Hawkins, "Tours and Tablets," *The Inkwell* (blog), accessed January 3, 2021, http://blogs.aaslh.org/tours-and-tablets/.
7. Lisa Junkin Lopez, "Introduction, 'Open House: Reimagining the Historic House Museum,'" *The Public Historian* 37, no. 2 (2015): 11.
8. Jennifer Scott, "Reimagining Freedom in the Twenty-first Century at a Post-Emancipation Site," *The Public Historian* 37, no. 2 (2015): 73–88.
9. "Slavery at Jefferson's Monticello: Paradox of Liberty," Paradox of Liberty, accessed January 3, 2021, https://www.monticello.org/ slavery/paradox-of-liberty/.
10. Franklin D. Vagnone and Deborah E. Ryan, *Anarchist's Guide to Historic House Museums* (California: Left Coast Press, 2016).
11. Potvin, "House or Home?," 10.
12. Benjamin Filene, "Passionate Histories: 'Outside' History-Makers and What They Teach Us," *The Public Historian* 34, no. 1 (Winter 2012): 11–33.
13. Rosenzweig and Thelen, *The Presence of the Past*, 89–104.
14. Plato, *Meno* 86b.
15. Lonnie G. Bunch III, "In Museums at the National Level: Fighting the Good Fight," in *Public History: Essays from the Field*, ed. James B.

Gardner and Peter S. LaPaglia (Florida: Krieger Publishing Company, 1999), 352.

15. My Autobiography of 'My Autobiography of Carson McCullers' by Jenn Shapland

1. Jenn Shapland, *My Autobiography of Carson McCullers* (Oregon: Tinn House, 2020), 59.
2. Shapland, *My Autobiography,* 59.
3. Shapland, *My Autobiography,* 99.
4. Shapland, *My Autobiography,* 79.
5. Shapland, *My Autobiography,* 105.
6. Shapland, *My Autobiography,* 40.
7. Shapland, *My Autobiography,* 26.

16. The Possibilities of Museum-as-Rhizome

1. "In Transit 2021 Call for Submissions," *Fwd: Museums Journal,* accessed January 3, 2021, https://fwdmuseumsjournal.weebly.com/in-transit-2021.html.
2. Gilles Deleuze and Félix Guattari, *A Thousand Plateaus: Capitalism and Schizophrenia* (Minneapolis: University of Minnesota Press, 1987): 10.
3. Deleuze and Guattari, 7.
4. Deleuze and Guattari, 21.
5. Elizabeth Adams St Pierre, "Writing as Post Qualitative Inquiry," *Qualitative Inquiry* 24, no. 9 (2018): 607. https://doi.org/10.1177/1077800417734567.
6. Dagmar Alexander and Jonathan Wyatt, "In(tra)fusion: Kitchen Research Practices, Collaborative Writing and Re-conceptualising The Interview," *Qualitative Inquiry* 24, no. 2 (2018), https://doi.org/10.1177/1077800416686370; Sarah Bridges-Rhoads, "Philosophical Fieldnotes." *Qualitative Inquiry* 24, no. 9 (2018), https://doi.org/10.1177/1077800417733498; Aaron M. Kuntz and Kelly W. Guyotte, "Inquiry on the Sly: Playful Intervention as Philosophical Action," *Qualitative Inquiry* 24, no. 9 (2018), https://doi.org/10.1177/1077800417734566.
7. Kuntz and Guyotte, 669.
8. "Art in Action", *MIMA,* accessed January 3, 2021, https://mima.art/art-in-action.
9. Jennifer Greene, "On Rhizomes, Lines Of Flight, Mangles, and Other Assemblages," *International Journal of Qualitative Studies in*

Education 26, no. 6 (2013): 751, https://doi.org/10.1080/09518398.2013.788763.

10. Susan N. Nordstrom, "Antimethodology: Postqualitative Generative Conventions," *Qualitative Inquiry* 24, no. 3 (2018): 216, https://doi.org/10.1177/1077800417704469.

11. L.M.M. Vieira and M. Ferasso, "The Rhizomatic Structure of Cyberspace: Virtuality and its Possibilities," *International Journal of Networking and Virtual Organisations* 7, no. 6 (2010): 553. https://dx.doi.org/10.1504/IJNVO.2010.035405.

12. Vieira and Ferasso, 553.

13. Vieira and Ferasso, 556.

14. Vieira and Ferasso, 554.

15. Vieira and Ferasso, 553.

16. *The White Pube*, accessed January 3, 2021, https://www.thewhitepube.co.uk/; *Death to Museums* archive, https://youtube.com/channel/UCiLyLYvXIWghzWezCjZEJXQ.

17. Nordstrom, 215–226.

18. Elizabeth Adams St Pierre, "Post Qualitative Inquiry, the Refusal of Method, and the Risk of the New," *Qualitative Inquiry* 27, no. 1 (2019): 4, https://doi.org/10.1177/1077800419863005.

19. Deleuze and Guattari, 8.

20. Greene, 753.

21. Deleuze and Guattari, 16–17.

22. Vieira and Ferasso, 557.

17. What if Museums Worked Like Libraries?

1. alliedmedia, "Writing New Worlds," Allied Media Conference, streamed live on July 24, 2020, Youtube video, 1:50:59, https://www.youtube.com/watch?v=i27YaBjzYqY.

2. Robin Wall Kimmerer, *Braiding Sweetgrass: Indigenous Wisdom, Scientific Knowledge and the Teachings of Plants* (London: Penguin Books, 2020), 4.

3. Christina Sharpe, *In the Wake: On Blackness and Being* (Durham: Duke University Press, 2016), 3.

4. Death to Museums, "Death To Museums January Session," streamed live on January 2, 2021, Youtube Video, 2:04:55, https://www.youtube.com/watch?v=iB9S4ccpGY0.

5. Drew, *This Is What I Know About Art,* (New York: Penguin Books, 2020); Sedgwick, "Paranoid Reading and Reparative Reading; or, You're So Paranoid, You Probably Think This Introduction is About You," in *Novel Gazing: Queer Readings in Fiction*, ed. Eve Kosofsky Sedgwick, (Durham: Duke University Press, 1997), 1–37.

18. Always Moving Forward

1. Memories of South Asia Facebook Group, Facebook, August 4, 2020. https://www.facebook.com/groups/memoriesofsouthasia.
2. Vazira Fazila-Yacoobali Zamindar, *The Long Partition and the Making of Modern South Asia: Refugees, Boundaries, Histories*, Cultures of History (New York: Columbia University Press, 2007).
3. Gerard Corsane, ed., *Heritage, Museums and Galleries: An Introductory Reader* (London: Routledge, 2005), 204.
4. C. Linde, *Working the Past: Narrative and Institutional Memory* (Oxford: Oxford University Press, 2009), 3–15.
5. Alessandro Portelli, *The Death of Luigi Trastulli, and Other Stories: Form and Meaning in Oral History*, (Albany: State University of New York Press, 1991); Paul Thompson, *The Voice of the Past: Oral History*, 3rd ed (Oxford: Oxford University Press, 2000).
6. Linde, *Working the Past*, 3–15.
7. Corsane, *Heritage, Museums and Galleries*, 204.

2022 CALL FOR SUBMISSIONS

MANIFESTO.

a declaration put into writing

the catalyst to spark a plan of action, to inspire change

to consider the present circumstance and announce its passing

to critique how something is and what it could be

To manifest is to put beyond question or doubt; to display; to exhibit.

How do you manifest yourself?

We accept any type of submission that explores this theme of MANIFESTO. Tell us your stories, ideas, declarations, and revelations of rejecting present circumstances and launching into a new era.

Possible Topics include:

Protest & revolution

Boundaries & dreams

Counter public(s)

Public engagement

Racial justice & accountability

Unionization

Fair wages

Anti-commodity

Access & accessibility

• Accessible, inclusive, & non-academic language

• How the pandemic has affected accessibility (to museums, ideas, communities)

• Unwelcoming physical & digital spaces

Political movements

Latin: Manifestus

Trauma in museums

How social movements shape museums

Museum Jobs physically/emotionally

• Exhausting museum jobs

• Meaningful work for everyone

Care & Care-work

• Care communities/collectives

• Making people feel comfortable

How can we be better artists?

How to come out on the other side post-COVID?

Deadline: January 5, 2022 by 11:59 (CT)—Submit art and texts here: shorturl.at/juN56

Questions? Email us: fwd.museums@gmail.com

Fwd: Museums invites academic articles, artwork, essays, exhibition/book reviews, creative writing, interviews, poetry, love letters, and other experimental forms to analyze, critique, and make space for new thinking about museums and exhibitions.

All submissions should follow the guidelines and relate to the journal's mission statement (see above). We strongly encourage book and exhibition reviews on multiple topics, but require all other submissions to connect to the seventh issue's theme, "MANIFESTO."

Guidelines

Written submissions should be between 1,000 and 2,500 words and use Chicago Manual of Style formatting and citations, in a DOCX file.

All images should be sent as separate files (not embedded in text) at 300+ dpi in tiff format. Note in text where images should be inserted and include credit, caption, date of execution, materials used, and dimensions, as appropriate.

A Note on Reviews

Reviews need not directly engage an issue's theme but should relate to the journal's mission statement (see below). We welcome long-form museum, exhibition, film, and book reviews with a point of view and connections to social, historical, political and other contexts. Check our

Instagram—@fwd_museums—for books available for review.

Who Should Submit?

Students, faculty, scholars, museum employees, artists and art handlers, volunteers, part-timers, activists, and other people with something to say about museums, exhibits, and cultural work are welcome to submit.

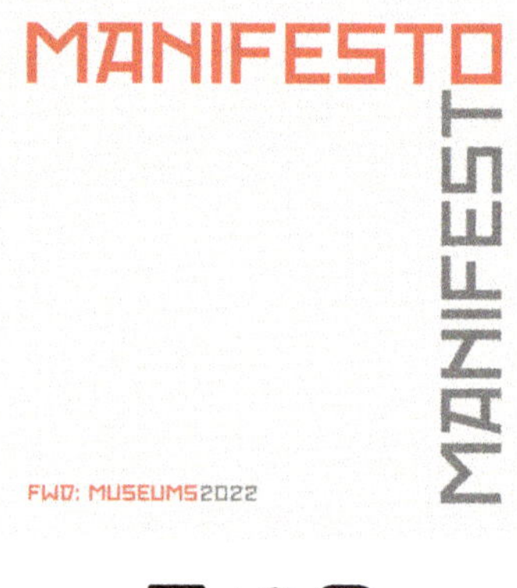